I0622736

Craving Spring

A mother's quest, a daughter's depression, and the Greek myth that brought them together

Ann Batchelder

Legacy Book Press LLC
Camanche, Iowa

ISBN: 979-8-9874823-1-5

Library of Congress Case Number: 1-12888616183

PRAISE FOR CRAVING SPRING

"*Craving Spring* starts with a fire, which is both metaphoric and real, transformative and damaging. It starts with a mother and a daughter, both (like all of us) flawed, both in a hospital, both ill in their own ways, joined by a spectral presence who may or may not actually be there. It is a memoir that circles around the question of what it is to be a parent, whether we can ever do it right, whether the best we can do is keep showing up for it. It is, in the end, a hard-won journey toward radical acceptance, and the power of simply asking another human being for help—in its simplicity it is incredibly moving."

—Nick Flynn, award-winning author of *Another Bullshit Night in Suck City* and *This is the Night Our House Will Catch Fire: A Memoir*

"A mythical, powerful, and true story of a mother's heroic journey home to her own heart as she comes face-to-face with her daughter's addiction. Ann Batchelder has expressed something extraordinary with relevance and profound teachings for any person who has ever sought to be free and to live life fully. This is a story of triumph. I highly recommend it."

—Tommy Rosen, Founder of Recovery 2.0

"Beautifully written, *Craving Spring* is a gut-wrenching yet uplifting story. It traces a mother's attempt to understand her daughter's struggles and find the answers to two questions most parents ask: *Why is this happening?* and *Am I good enough?*"

—Jay Cutspec, Director of Health and Counseling, UNC-Asheville

"This is a gripping tale that elegantly illustrates the relevance of the ancient Greek myth of Demeter and Persephone to modern-day mother–daughter struggles. A masterful storyteller, Ann Batchelder takes us deep into the heart of a mother's love while demonstrating the power of myth to illuminate a path toward healing. This book is a gift to anyone trying to navigate the complexities of the mother–daughter relationship."

—Anita Johnston, Ph.D., psychologist and author of *Eating in the Light of the Moon: How Women Can Transform Their Relationships with Food Through Myths, Metaphors, and Storytelling*

"I loved this book for hundreds of reasons. Ann Batchelder's brilliant memoir unearths the dank truths about a mother's needs when her child is suffering. *Craving Spring* shows us how to untangle maternal judgment to access love and create meaningful relationships with our kids and ourselves."

—Loren Greiff, Founder of PortfolioRocket

"With crisp sentences and thriller-like pacing, Ann Batchelder has crafted an unforgettable book about a mother's desperate quest to save her troubled daughter—and herself. *Craving Spring* is so deeply heartfelt that I felt it in my own heart, often pounding as I read—and yet I could not put it down."

—Lynn Melnick, author of *I've Had to Think Up a Way to Survive: On Trauma, Persistence, and Dolly Parton*

for Olivia

Compassion is not a relationship between the healer and the wounded. It's a relationship between equals. Only when we know our own darkness well can we be present with the darkness of others. Compassion becomes real when we recognize our shared humanity.

—Pema Chödrön

Author's Note

Everything in this book happened, but as with all memoirs, I offer my perspective of those events. For privacy, some names are pseudonyms; most are not. The chapters titled "Demeter (Re-imagined)" are based on Gregory Nagy's translation of the *Homeric Hymn to Demeter*. There are many interpretations of this ancient Greek myth. Homer, thought to have been an oral poet around the Archaic Period, 8th century BCE, is credited with the original story. Scribes would have written down his song (either during or after his lifetime), altering or embellishing each version. We are all mythmakers. As Pema Chödrön said, "The future is completely open, and we are writing it moment to moment."

Table of Contents

Part One

The Man from Spain

A man stands against the wall in my daughter's room at Vanderbilt Hospital. I call him *Malvado*. He wears no shirt, just a thin raincoat hanging from his shoulders. It is frayed and stinks of backstreet garbage and days-old sweat, but he doesn't care. Taking a long drag from his cigarette, he exhales toward the ceiling then squints at me, his eyes like two black lines carved into a bald head. I try to ignore him, pretending not to notice his ashes dropping onto the floor. He knows he's not supposed to smoke in a burn unit. He knows other things, too. He knows what kind of mother I am. If I'd been different, perhaps none of this would have happened.

The potent odor of disinfectant barely covers the stench of scorched flesh and misery pervading the unit. I'm waiting for my daughter, Olivia, to return from surgery. It's taking a long time, or maybe it isn't. I sit erect on the edge of a stiff vinyl recliner wedged into a corner, my hands clenched in my lap. I watch a young boy standing in the hallway, his body covered with burn marks, his face disfigured. The nurse next to him bends down to say something. Her eyes are sad but unflinching. She's used to seeing patients who are scarred and scared. I look away.

I notice I haven't taken off my coat. Next to me, two tall windows are sealed shut against a cloudy February day, but I can still feel the cold. Forcing myself to take a deep breath, I scan the cramped room. There's a minuscule sink, a narrow tray on wheels, a TV hanging from the ceiling. The large monitor next to Olivia's bed keeps beeping. I wonder if it can offer any order to the unpredictable incidents that brought my daughter here.

A nurse appears. She tells me Olivia is getting her leg wrapped and should be arriving soon. The nurse doesn't see Malvado—he is invisible to everyone but me. Maybe he is a shade, a ghost. Maybe a fiend. When he first began to haunt me, I'd try to make him disappear by squeezing my eyes shut. Later, I would scream at him, "What did I do to deserve this? What did she?" But he wouldn't answer, and he wouldn't go away. Instead, he took up residence within me, infecting my thoughts—a cancer of the soul.

Lately, he seems to be everywhere. At night, while I'm still awake in bed, I often catch a whiff of cigarette smoke coming from the dark edge of the bedroom. It's him, daring me to sleep so he can sabotage my dreams. Sometimes, when I'm driving, I'll get a glimpse of him in the rearview mirror. And when I am on the phone, confessing to friends how confused or frightened I am about my daughter, I can tell he's eavesdropping, rolling his eyes. I don't have to wonder what he's thinking. His wordless judgments slip into my brain and twist around until they are tight and true.

My daughter is wheeled into the room, her left leg encased in a huge bandage from the knee down. She's mysteriously beautiful, like a Vermeer painting, her green eyes large and wistful. Easing herself onto the bed, Olivia props her burned leg on top of three pillows and gives me a weak smile. At twenty years old, she has already experienced a lifetime of pain, but she is still a child, my child.

"Hey, Olivia." I lean over to hug her.

"Thanks for being here, Mom. I guess I did want you to come after all."

"Next time we have a mother–daughter get-together, let's pick someplace like Paris instead of a hospital."

"Yeah, I know. Right?" She laughs. I laugh. It's a stupid joke. She takes a long look out the window and starts to tear up. I reach to hold her hand.

"So, how are you doing?" I ask.

"It hurts. This whole thing sucks, actually."

"You mean your burn?"

"I mean all of it, Mom." Malvado walks over to the window and leans against it, waiting to hear what I will say next—what brilliant words of wisdom, what consoling comments, what motherly advice. But I have nothing, and he knows it.

The Descent

I hadn't always been unsure of myself as a mother. I thought I was doing everything right. My husband Henri and I had moved to a rural area outside Asheville, North Carolina, to raise our two young children. I dubbed this period in our family's history the "Huckleberry Finn Years." In the spring and fall, we'd spend a lot of time outdoors hiking and having picnics along the Blue Ridge Parkway. In winter, we'd play broom hockey together on the frozen pond below our house. And on the long drives to grade school, I'd give the kids "Mom's music history lessons," and we'd sing our way from Buddy Holly to the Beach Boys to the Beatles.

Olivia and her older brother, Austin, learned to catch lizards and fireflies and little ring-necked snakes. They also learned how to get along if they wanted a playmate. Despite the four-year difference, they rarely fought. He was gentle and patient. She was feisty and willing to try anything.

On Sundays, when the weather was warm, I decided we should have "home church," because none of us wanted to dress up and drive twenty minutes to town. I wasn't particularly religious. I'd studied religion in high school and college, read a lot of books by Buddhist teachers like Pema Chödrön and Tara Brach, did yoga (off and on), and tried to meditate. Still, I felt it was important to educate my children about Bible stories so they could appreciate Renaissance art, teach them the Lord's Prayer so they'd have something to say if the plane went down, and remind them how to sing a song of thanks. So, in our pajamas, Austin, Olivia, and I walked down to the pond, sat on the dock, lit a candle, and conducted our brief ceremony. Then, we hiked back up the hill to join Henri, who'd be busy making pancakes in the kitchen.

When Olivia finished middle school, we moved into town and built a house on a bluff. Henri and I worked well as a team, and we loved the process of creating a comfortable home for our family. We'd decided that the house would be modern without feeling rigid or sterile, and it had to have a view. This was especially important to me. Having grown up in the flatlands of Illinois, I longed to be perched up high so I could wonder what was just beyond the horizon and watch the seasons change. Our floor-to-ceiling living room windows overlooked a lush valley with downtown Asheville and waves of soft mountains in the distance.

Among the oldest mountains in the world, the Appalachians once stood as high as the Alps. Whittled down to their essence after millions of years, they'd become smaller, wiser. We lived within the hills of Western North Carolina for twenty-two years, worked and raised our children there, and gathered our community. Whenever I gazed out our windows, I felt revived and comforted, imagining the ancient knowledge lying deep within those gentle blue ridges.

The first year living in our new house was a sweet time for our family. Olivia was a freshman and Austin a senior in high school. I often heard them upstairs giggling about school gossip or watching movies together. After Austin went to college, he was rarely home. A whitewater kayaker and dedicated athlete, he spent every summer in Europe competing in races, hoping to earn a spot on the U.S. Olympic Kayak Development Team. Even during Thanksgiving, Austin's coach took the athletes to Mexico to practice in warmer rivers. Christmas became the only holiday our family spent together. I realized it would only be a few short years before Olivia would be off to college, too. With that in mind, I'd begun thinking about the impending empty-nest stage. "It's like getting a pink slip from my mothering job," I told a friend.

Most days, I felt just fine about my life, content and anchored—like on that warm, late afternoon in 2009. It was a Wednesday in July. I was home alone, preparing a spaghetti dinner. I'd finished curating a major contemporary art exhibition for the museum in Asheville earlier that spring and appreciated having some time to myself before starting a consulting business helping artists and creative entrepreneurs.

Henri had called earlier that day saying he had a meeting at the hospital and would be late. Olivia, freshly sixteen, was a rising high school junior. I expected her to be home soon for dinner. She was volunteering for a month on an archeological project organized by a local college. The dig, an ancient Native American site, was forty-five minutes from our house in Asheville. I was a bit nervous about her driving alone into the countryside along narrow roads, far from cell service and towns, but Henri assured me she would be fine.

The first day Olivia went to the dig, she got lost. Not wanting to be late, she stepped on her gas pedal. Then, a state trooper stepped on his. By the time he finished filling out her ticket, she was too embarrassed and upset to go to the dig, so she slinked home and took a nap.

"It could happen to anyone," her father had told her. "You have to watch your speedometer coming down the hills. I know that stretch of road. The cops are always there." Henri usually gave our kids the benefit of the doubt. He reminded me that teenagers make mistakes, and I relied on his sense of fairness. After tears, apologies, and a lecture on driving safety, Henri and I decided to let the subject drop. We wanted to give her a break.

High school had not been easy for Olivia. At first, she'd been excited to try new things, but field hockey was a disappointment, and so was the debate team. As a result, she'd spent her first year fluctuating between friends and activities, searching for a way to belong. Her sophomore year had been challenging in another way. Olivia hated the idea of being the only child at home. Just before Austin left for college, as we were finishing a family dinner, Olivia turned to him and said, "You're leaving me with THEM?" Austin immediately pretended to choke, spitting out his water, and everyone laughed. He was quick to defuse any family tension with comedic comebacks, and we were always relieved.

After Austin left home, our family dinners weren't the same. Too many times, we struggled to find a common language. Too often, Henri defaulted to grilling Olivia about her homework just to fill the silence, then I would tell him to be quiet, which only made him angry. Sometimes, the tension in the air between us cracked open. Henri and I would start bickering over everything and nothing until one of us left the table, abruptly ending dinner.

Summers, on the other hand, were looser, lovelier, lazier. We were unhurried, unpressured. Henri and Olivia worshipped the warm months. Beginning with the summer solstice, as each passing day brought us closer to the dark and cold, they bemoaned the return of winter. But darkness arrived early that summer.

While my meatball sauce simmered, a lovely diffusion of sautéed onions and fresh mountain air flowed through the house. Over the sound system speakers, Maria Callas was singing "Violetta's Aria" from Verdi's *La Traviata*, an opera about a woman who'd been led astray by the cruelties of life. I secretly believed such mournful, sensuous music would help spice up my Italian meal. I also loved how Maria used her voice. She wasn't afraid of the dissonant notes. Instead, she'd hold them a little longer, swelling the phrase with tension and passion, making the resolution that much sweeter. With no one listening, I wanted to see if I could trust my voice to follow her. Cranking up the volume a bit, I tried to sing along.

The sun was seriously thinking about setting, its honey-colored warm bands of light slowly shifting across the green treetops beyond our deck. The afternoon was giving itself to evening just as Maria Callas was reaching her crescendo. As I took in a deep breath to join her, I heard Olivia crunch the family Prius onto our gravel driveway—a bit too fast, I noted. The spell with Maria was broken, but I didn't care. I was looking forward to hearing about Olivia's day at the dig.

The back screen door slammed, then there was silence—no *hello*, no teenager clomping into the house, slinging her purse on the kitchen counter, as usual. Nothing. It was as if she'd vaporized. I peered around the corner in time to see her slim body slowly slide down the doorframe and collapse, exhausted, onto the floor. Maria Callas couldn't have done it better. I bent over and was about to make a joke when I saw her face had seized into a painful grimace—she was a crumpled tangle of long hair, hoop earrings, blue jeans shorts, halter top, and tears. Dropping to the floor, I gently gripped her thin shoulders and peered into her face.

"What's wrong? What happened?"

Choking for air, she tried to speak but couldn't. I wrapped her in my arms for what seemed like a very long time. I instinctively knew to wait. Olivia was a sensitive kid and comfortable expressing a wide range of emotions, but this was different. Staring up at me with swollen eyes, she tried to speak, but her body gave way again to anguished sobs.

She's frightened, not sad, I thought. The muscles in my back tightened against whatever terrible news she needed to tell me. Had one of her friends died in a car accident? All I knew was she was safe now with me. I waited and gently rocked her, whispering into her ear as one would to a small child or wounded animal—asking her to take a breath, telling her she was okay. Then, she spoke.

"The past two days, I've thought about driving my car into a tree, and I almost did it today. I came home as fast as I could. I was so scared, Mom."

My heart seemed to stop. Olivia was crying again, and I kept rocking us both like I hadn't heard what she said. None of it made sense. An onslaught of questions kept scrambling my brain, making it impossible for my mouth to form words.

"And there's more," she said, pulling away just far enough to look at me. "I've been throwing up."

"Oh, I'm so sorry. Are you sick?"

"No, Mom. I mean, I eat a lot, then I make myself throw up." For a moment, I couldn't breathe. Fearful of what she might say next, I forced myself to remain very, very still.

"How long have you been doing this?" I finally asked, almost too casually.

"Most of the year, but every day since April." That's when I felt the floor beneath us start to give way, exposing a dark pit below. Holding each other, we seemed to be floating, suspended over a bottomless cavern of despair. If I let go of her, we might both fall into it forever. I held her tighter.

I felt my heart violently pumping, blood rushing up my neck, the pressure throbbing in my ears. If Maria was still singing, I could no longer hear her. I had no clue what to do or say next and cursed myself for being so inept and afraid. Then, like a newborn colt, Olivia unfolded her legs and stood up. Wobbly at first, she walked into the kitchen. I followed, extending my arm to rub her back, but she moved just out of reach.

"I'm going upstairs now to take a nap. I'm tired," Olivia said over her shoulder. I went to the stove and stared into the simmering pot. It gave me somewhere to go, something to do.

Could she honestly think of killing herself? I wondered. The spoon in my hand kept stirring the red sauce in circles. I watched the steam rise as tears fell into the pot. Olivia seemed happy when she was young. When did things change?

Olivia

That night, as I was lying in bed, thinking about Olivia, I felt like I was on stage, facing a thousand eyes. The audience in my head was waiting for me to sing, but I had no idea what the song was supposed to be. The muscles around my windpipe tightened. My fluttering heart sent electric currents up and down my arms. Sweat was soaking my nightshirt.

What happened to her? I asked myself over and over. I kept scanning my memory for clues. What bitter set of circumstances had poisoned my daughter? Was it the depression that ran in Henri's family? Did living under the shadow of her older brother make her feel deficient? Had the skinny kids in her dance troupe caused her to lose confidence, or was it the bitchy fifth-grade girls who'd bullied her in private grade school? Was she trying too hard to keep up with the wilder crowd in high school? Should we have given her more chores growing up?

Was it my fault?

As a child, Olivia dreamed of being free. She'd hoped to become a princess one day, relieved of her mundane life. Every Halloween, she'd try on a different Disney persona and pretend to be Arial or Mulan or Jasmine. Once, on vacation, when Olivia was nine years old, our family signed up for an afternoon horseback ride along the beach. Olivia insisted on riding up front with the guide. She naturally sat tall in the saddle with her jaw thrust forward in a regal manner. When the group approached the sand, Olivia's horse took off, galloping along the shoreline. The guide raced after her as the rest of us watched in horror. When he caught up to Olivia, she was laughing. She later told us she'd never felt so alive.

On days when she could no longer tolerate being a kid, she'd become defiant. I remember one cold, rainy morning, after I drove her to kindergarten, we sat in the parking lot having a heated debate about her raincoat. The more I insisted she take it, the more she dug in her heels and refused. I wasn't about to give in, and neither was she. She finally agreed but slammed the car door and stormed up the steps to school. A mother standing nearby looked at me and raised her eyebrows.

"Sorry. She's not easy, huh?" she said. This woman's daughter was timid as a mouse. Although I was mad at Olivia, I wasn't about to let her pass judgment on my kid so easily.

I smiled. "She's tough all right," I said. "Hard for mom but good for her."

The fact was, I was envious of Olivia, and maybe I let her get away with being irreverent too often. She vented her frustration in ways I was never allowed to at her age, but she could also be a delight. She expressed her love with equal abandon. Sometimes, for no apparent reason, she'd walk up to me and throw her arms around my neck in a tight embrace, and I'd wonder how I could be so lucky to have such a daughter.

Strong and capable, always smiling and willing to pitch in, Olivia was the kind of kid camp counselors loved. When someone told a joke, she'd throw her head back and explode with laughter. As a young child, she'd dress up in costumes with long beads and hats to sing and dance around the house. Her world was dramatic and fun.

Once she got to fourth grade, though, Olivia seemed to shrink. She became hesitant at school and embarrassed that she needed extra reading help because she had a learning difference. She didn't understand social rules and often found herself alone. I remember seeing her on the playground, grabbing friends from behind to give them bear hugs. Her affections weren't always returned. The other kids seemed more bewildered than amused.

As the years progressed and friendships at school eluded her, she found the joy of self-expression in modern dance. Her dance studio was a place where she could be herself. She was a muscular dancer, grounded to the Earth, not an airy ballerina. In performances, she would captivate audiences by gracefully vacillating between control and abandon, letting her body tell the stories of her heart. She had hopes of majoring in dance but developed scoliosis during puberty. The pain in her back forced her to quit the junior company she'd been performing with for years.

A creative soul, my daughter was also restless, always eager to get to the next stage of life. She even came out of the womb in a hurry. Once I started having hard labor, Olivia was born in seventeen minutes. She was like a stallion kept too long in a pasture. I'd try to tell her to slow down, but I knew she wanted to jump the fence. In 2007, at age fifteen, she found an opportunity.

Olivia spent the summer volunteering on the island of Dominica in the Caribbean. The program organized high school students from the United States to help paint community buildings and re-thatch roofs. Even though Olivia contracted mono and bronchitis while volunteering, she never complained. She said it was one of the best summers she'd ever had because she felt needed.

That Christmas, when Olivia was fifteen, I asked her if she wanted to go with me to Obama's inauguration in early January. "It'll be fun," I said. "We can drive there together and visit family along the way." I knew Olivia cared about Obama's election. She had a giant poster of him on her bedroom wall, among photos of dancers, snapshots of her friends, and handwritten poems. I wanted her to feel like she was a part of history. When I was her age, I was too young to go on my own to Washington, D.C., to march against the Vietnam War. And I'd just missed going to Woodstock.

It was cold but sunny the day we were putting things in the car, preparing for our journey. Underneath an armful of bangles, I saw a design on Olivia's wrist I'd noticed before. It was not unusual for her to draw doodles on the back of her hands or above her knee.

"Why don't you wash that off before we leave," I'd said. "It's been there long enough." I even took her arm, licked my finger, and tried to rub it off myself.

"Mom, it's a tattoo."

"What? How did you get that?" I asked, still trying to rub it off. "It's illegal in North Carolina to get a tattoo until you're eighteen." In 2009, no one I knew had high school children with tattoos. Anyone tattooing a juvenile could be charged with a misdemeanor for "contributing to the delinquency of a minor."

"I got it last summer when I was in the Caribbean. We all did." I stared at her wrist, shocked that I'd been in denial about her "drawing" for the past six months.

"Look—it's an interlacing circle," Olivia said. "I worked a long time on the design. It reminds me of never-ending friendship." I peered closer and saw the entangled beauty of it, but I couldn't admit that. I didn't want her to run out and get another one.

"But it's permanent!" I said, trying to hold back my anger, realizing her young skin would forever have this mark. "Olivia, we talked about this. You knew your father and I wouldn't approve."

Olivia shrugged as if to say, *What's done is done.* She shrugged later when we made her get tested for AIDS in case the needles the tattoo artist used weren't clean. And she shrugged when one of her teachers made a negative comment about her tattoo.

Toward the end of her sophomore year, Olivia decided to quit playing on the school field hockey team and shrugged when her grades started to slip. Rather than trying to be a perfect student like her brother, she focused on being cool. She became obsessed with finding a boyfriend, obsessed with how her body looked, obsessed with fitting in. I heard from a few of my friends who had kids in Olivia's class that she'd been drinking at parties, but I didn't have firsthand knowledge to confront her, only rumors.

Then, something deeper shifted in Olivia. She seemed raw and sensitive to every slight, every sideways glance. And she was often in tears. Nothing seemed right. At night, she'd often lock herself in her bathroom for hours. Sometimes, I'd knock on the door to ask if she wanted to talk, but she'd tell me she was fine. When I'd drive her to school in the mornings, she kept the music loud or said she was too sleepy for conversation.

I was at a loss about how to reach Olivia. Growing up, my mother never encouraged me to talk about my problems. I kept hoping Olivia's struggles were not unusual, that she was a sensitive teenager having a tough year. But now, my daughter was telling me she was suicidal. I wasn't prepared for this.

First Lessons in Motherhood

My childhood had been bland as milk toast. I grew up in Peoria in the middle of nowhere in the middle of Illinois. My Midwest grandparents hadn't survived horrendous conditions in some old country. One day, they just sprang up alongside the monolithic rows of corn that reached forever to the flat horizon. Few surprises came with this lot. To be boring and normal was an honorable family pursuit. As a result, my two much older brothers and I kept any unpleasantness hidden from the world and each other. No one admitted mistakes. Open discussions were not encouraged, and complaining was not allowed. I remember when I was six years old, my father scolded me for crying. Taking hold of my arm, he gave me a quick but firm shake that startled me.

"Old soldiers don't cry," he'd said. He was a big, no-nonsense kind of guy, a successful businessman, and a veteran of World War II. He was not to be crossed.

This was the late 1950s. My parents often hosted lavish cocktail parties for their country club friends at our house. The men arrived in sports coats and ties and usually had both off before the end of the night. The women wore tight dresses in peach pink, buttercup yellow, or robin's egg blue. One night, when the guests were amply lubricated, they gathered around the piano and urged my mother to perform.

After a few tunes to get things going, Mom played her favorite torch song, Billie Holiday's "I Cried for You." But rather than sing with despair, she belted out this song with all the Ethel Merman force she could muster, growling out the word "cried." Then, for extra effect, she'd even yodel up an octave when she got to the end of the line: "I criiiiied for yoooo-hoo." Everyone around the piano laughed.

I learned that night that music could be a code language. My mother choosing to sing about letting go of a cheating man was the only hint I had that something wasn't right with my parents' marriage. I wonder, now, if her friends knew. My father seemed oblivious to her feelings as he egged her on to sing another song. Through the rest of the night, she'd pummel the black and white keys, singing so loudly I could make out every angry word as I tried to sleep on the other end of the house—upstairs in my pink wallpapered bedroom, with the door shut and a pillow over my head.

When I was young, Mom and I made up a game called "Name that Tune." She'd play melodies on the piano from her college years in the 1930s—like "Moon Indigo" or "Stardust" or "Moonlight Serenade." These songs, written to be wispy and romantic, my mother played with gusto. I didn't care. Our game was one of the few activities we shared. I loved watching her sturdy hands tap dance up and down the keyboard. She'd throw in a minor seventh chord, then experiment with other black keys, coaxing the notes to live close together and still be harmonic. If it didn't sound right, she'd try hammering the chord into submission as if playing the piano harder could fix things. I patiently sat beside her on the polished, slippery piano bench, eager for her praise, proudly guessing each song title as she pounded away.

Being able to fix things was the goal of just about everything my mother did. She repaired a leaky faucet with the same zeal she applied to managing her unhappy marriage. Problems, like dirty laundry, were not to be aired. And for a mother to be successful, she told me, it was up to the woman of the house to stay in control of her children. Otherwise, "it will be a sorry situation." I made a mental note to follow her lead when I became a mother.

For generations, women in my family lived by a strict rule predicated on a sixteenth-century Protestant idea: mothers were responsible for controlling their children's successes and failures. If all went as planned, the children would be happy. Then, and only then, the mother would be congratulated on a job well done, and she could relax.

My own experience with motherhood began in 1985. Henri and I were living in New York, where we'd met and married, when he was offered a position in a radiology practice in Asheville, North Carolina. Although

I loved my job at the Brooklyn Academy of Music, I was ready to leave the city and start a family. The move was an opportunity to establish our new life, though I never imagined I would one day be living south of the Mason-Dixon Line.

"Going to Asheville will be an adventure—like traveling to Asia," I joked to Henri after we'd made our decision. But we weren't tourists. We were moving for good. And once I got to North Carolina, I didn't enjoy being a stranger, or worse, a Yankee. In the mid-80s, Asheville was not just a small mountain town. It was broken and forgotten, a shell of a place that was once vibrant and prosperous. The city's shops stood abandoned, their windows boarded up with plywood. There were only a couple of places to eat, a movie theater known for showing porn, and at night the dark downtown streets were alive with rats.

Once we'd settled in Asheville, I got a job as editor of a magazine called *FIBERARTS* and became pregnant with Austin. My OB/GYN told me my pregnancy would be a challenge. My mother took a drug called DES when she was pregnant with me. It was commonly prescribed in the 1950s to prevent miscarriages. What doctors didn't realize at the time was that DES could wreak havoc on the reproductive organs of an offspring in utero. As a result, I was born with a small uterus, twisted fallopian tubes, and not much of a cervix.

Henri and I assumed everything would be fine with my pregnancy because my doctor had put a stitch in my cervix to baste it shut and keep our baby from falling out. But after examining me at our three-month check-up, the doctor snapped off his glove and shook his head.

"It doesn't look good," he said. "You need to go home right now. Get in bed and stay there. For the next six months, I only want you to get up to go to the bathroom." Henri and I stared at him, still waiting for good news.

"You won't be able to attend Lamaze classes," the doctor continued, "but you can arrange for a midwife to come to your house to give you a crash course on natural childbirth." He turned to throw the glove in the garbage and opened the office door.

"What about my job?" I asked.

"You have to decide if you want this baby or not," my doctor said. Henri put his arm around my shoulder, partly for support and partly, I felt, to keep me from taking a swing.

In New York, the women I knew were typically in partnership with their doctors regarding health care, respected as informed patients capable of meaningful interchanges. Not so in North Carolina. In the 1980s, most women in the South were still treated as if they were ignorant and somehow at fault for any sorry predicament in their lives. If you were stuck in a bad marriage, you should have known better than to marry someone like that in the first place. If you were raped, you must have done something stupid to become a victim.

As we left his office, my doctor reminded me that I was confined to bedrest because I had an "irritable bowel" and an "incompetent cervix."

"And a bitchy vagina, no doubt," I said under my breath.

Once home, Henri outfitted our bedroom with a compact refrigerator, small black-and-white TV, side table for my work files, and a landline phone. This was to be my world until our baby was born. I depended on Henri's confidence, efficiency, and love to get through each day. In the mornings, he'd wake me with a kiss and a backrub, bring me cereal and juice, and put a sandwich and carton of milk in the bedside refrigerator for my lunch. Then he'd leave for work, and I'd be alone all day.

At the magazine, we used to joke that personal computers hadn't yet made it over the mountains to Asheville. Cell phones, internet, and cable TV hadn't either. Lying sideways in bed, I did my job editing articles with a red pen. After squinting for several hours, the last thing I wanted to do was read a novel, so to entertain myself, I'd give solo concerts to the baby in my belly. I sang whatever came to mind, imagining the muffled music he heard while submerged within me. I often let loose on a blues song or one of the few opera pieces I knew. Like a big-chested diva, I filled my lungs with tenderness and longing, singing to heaven for relief, but the songs only reached the white popcorn ceiling of our rented house.

On the flip side of those long days, there were several harrowing, middle-of-the-night emergency trips to the hospital. Fearful of going into premature labor, I knew to tell Henri right away if I felt any tightening in my abdomen. He would hurry me to the car and speed us across town to the hospital. Somehow, a nurse always got IV fluids started just in time to slow the contractions.

The day Austin was born was the first time someone told me to "let go." After lying flat for six months trying to contain my baby in utero, I was finally ready to stand and deliver. I had returned to my hospital room after slowly and painfully walking up and down the hall with Henri—one of several attempts I'd made over eight hours to get our son born. Nothing was working. As I settled back onto the bed, I told Henri I would be fine and suggested he go downstairs to get something to eat. A few moments after he left, I felt a sharp pain followed by unrelenting cramps. Waves of contractions mounted, one after another. The pain, already more than I thought possible, was now more than I could bear.

"I think we should call the doctor and get my husband back here," I groaned. The nurse, a middle-aged woman with stringy hair tied up in a bun, was used to first-time mothers.

Touching my arm, she whispered, "Just let go and let God."

You're kidding, right? I thought. *What makes you think I even believe in God?* But rather than bite her head off, I gritted my teeth into what I thought might resemble a smile. "I think I'm ready to have those drugs now," I hissed. "Forget natural childbirth!"

"It's too late, dear. You're too far along for medication. You'll just have to hang in there," the nurse said. Her smile turned down just a bit.

I was pissed. *Why didn't someone tell me this might happen if I waited too long?* I wondered. *Why hadn't I been given the playbook on becoming a mother?*

The doctor came into the room to check on me, all smiles. First, he performed a physical exam. Glancing up at the baby's heart monitor next to me, he exhibited the same smile-turned-down the nurse was wearing.

They must teach people how to do that in the South, I marveled. Then Henri returned—a sandwich in one hand, Diet Coke in the other—and stood staring at the beeping machine, too. Everyone was silent. Something was alarming enough to make these three upbeat, cheery people stop smiling. The doctor sat down on my bed, taking his own deep breath.

"The umbilical cord is getting compressed behind the baby's neck. His heart is slowing down," he told me. "We have to do a Cesarean section right away."

I nodded, but before I could speak, the doctor stood up and started barking orders. Several nurses hurried into the room, slamming into each other around my bed, unhooking the monitors and preparing me for transit. No time to find a gurney. As someone wheeled me down the hallway, Henri raced next to the bed, pulling on sterile hospital scrubs.

The nurses shoved my bed through a pair of massive doors into an icy cold operating room. Henri, a doctor himself who was usually calm in an emergency, bent down into my face and whispered, "If you feel the need to push, then PUSH!" Seeing the look in his eyes, I understood we were in trouble. I could lose this baby right here, right now. I felt a contraction coming and began to bear down hard. The doctor, preparing to cut my belly open, whipped around to check my vagina one last time, then yelled at me over my bent knees.

"Whoa, whoa! Slow down a little!" he yelled. "You're pushing too hard." Blood was rushing out, and so was the baby. "The baby's head is crowning. It's coming too fast," he told the nurses. "We're not doing the Cesarean." Everyone in the operating room shifted to the lower end of the table, where I couldn't see what was going on. I stared up into the bright ceiling lights and forced myself to take deep breaths.

"Hold on if you can," the doctor instructed. "We have to get this baby out quickly, but we must be careful. His right elbow is up near his ear. You're getting torn from stem to stern."

I don't care, I said to myself, *just save my baby.*

I lost a lot of blood that day and had to have many internal and external stitches. My doctor called it a "vaginal Cesarean" birth. Had I not pushed, everyone told me, who knows what would have happened?

According to the ladies in my mother's Bible study group, I had delivered my first "miracle baby." Even my doctor told me I was courageous. Between the months of bedrest and the frightening delivery, it had been a long, arduous journey, and I was the heroine of the story.

"I did what any mother would do," I'd respond demurely, though secretly, I was pleased to be taking credit for a job well done. My son's difficult yet joyful birth was my first lesson in motherhood: my children's survival and happiness would be directly related to the level of sacrifice, determination, and control I provided for them. What kind of mother would ever want to let go?

The Hounds from Hades

I felt good about my mothering skills when our kids started high school because they were both "doing well." Austin made it easy for us to let him be independent. Because he was a serious athlete determined to go to the Olympics, he made the dean's list, never drank, and went to bed early, even on weekends. I assumed Olivia's path would be less conservative, but once she told me she had suicidal thoughts, everything changed. I went on high alert. It wasn't a question of not letting go. I had to fight for my child's life.

My first step was to become laser-focused on reading everything I could about eating disorders and depression. I'd review my findings with Henri in hopes we could gain insight into Olivia's self-destructive behavior.

"You should talk to people and figure out what we're supposed to do," Henri said one evening after reading another article I'd printed for him. "Call around and find an expert. I'll do whatever they say." Henri needed a plan, not research. He seemed immobilized by what was happening with Olivia. He'd worked hard in medical school so he could have a comfortable, uncomplicated life.

When Henri was eight years old, his father had committed suicide, leaving his mother to raise three boys with no money. For years, he, his mother, and two brothers often fought and struggled to get along. He desperately wanted to have a more stable family of his own. Having a teenage daughter in distress triggered his anxieties about having to face a family crisis. Henri was excellent at diagnosing MRI scans at work and advising other doctors concerning their patients' difficult predicaments, but when it came to emotional turmoil at home, he relied on me to handle things.

I was always happy to oversee our children's well-being. Because my work with the magazine was more flexible than Henri's job, I stayed home when the kids were sick and spent extra time helping with homework projects. I took them shopping for clothes and supplies, drove them to afterschool lessons and doctor appointments, packed their lunches and made dinner every night, volunteered at school, and orchestrated all the playdates. It seemed natural that I would also handle Olivia's bulimia and depression. I found the best adolescent psychiatrist in town to assist with depression medication and took her to an eating disorder therapist.

"You'll have to be with her to monitor everything she eats for breakfast, lunch, and dinner," the therapist told us at our first meeting. Olivia was sitting straight up, motionless. She didn't speak or move her head but looked over at me, her eyes wide, as if pleading with me to get us out of the room.

"You can't expect me to go to high school with her," I said.

"Well, then be sure you pack her lunch. After school, you should pick Olivia up and bring her straight home. She needs to stay with you until she goes to bed." Rather than allowing Olivia more independence, I was supposed to treat my teenage daughter like a grade school kid. I held my hands together into a tight ball, refusing to return Olivia's glare.

"How long are we supposed to do this?" I asked.

"It will take a while, I expect. Most people with eating disorders struggle for years to recover until they find the right tools. For now, we're just trying to break the cycle of using food in an unhealthy way." I didn't like the sound of this. Olivia couldn't suffer "for years." It seemed up to me to get her better—sooner rather than later.

At first, Olivia was compliant and relieved to be getting help. When Austin was briefly in Asheville that summer, I mentioned that his sister was working through some eating disorder issues. "She's depressed," I told him, hoping that answer would be sufficient.

"But what's wrong with her?" He waited for my answer, his eyes steady on me, his lips tight.

"I'm not sure, but she'll be fine. She's working with a therapist."

"I could hear her last night when I went to bed. She was in the bathroom, crying to someone on the phone. It seems like there's always some big drama going on lately. This isn't right, Mom." After he'd left for college, Austin and Olivia headed in very different directions. He told me that he wasn't so sure about some of her friends, who seemed to take more risks than the kids he knew.

"It's hard," I said. "She just needs time. It wasn't always easy for you in high school, either." I knew I was running interference, not wanting him to judge her. I felt like a puppeteer frantically trying to keep our family dancing as if nothing was wrong backstage. Plus, I didn't have the energy to take care of Austin's emotions in that moment, so I downplayed the problem. I didn't tell him about the piles of candy wrappers I found squirreled away under her pillow and in the back of her closet. I was embarrassed for her when I lifted the toilet seat and realized she'd thrown up, so I'd clean it without saying a word. I figured there wasn't much Austin could do about it anyway. We didn't discuss his sister's problem again that summer, just tiptoed around it.

Once school started, Olivia did her homework at the dining table while Henri and I monitored her. This was also meant to distract her from her anxiety, the feeling that something wasn't right with her. It didn't help. Night after night, the tension in our house mounted, often resulting in tearful standoffs.

One evening after dinner, Olivia announced she was going up to her room. "I promise, I'll be fine," she said. "You don't have to worry about me."

"I'm sorry, but you can't leave," I said. "You have to stay downstairs for an hour."

"Damn it. Just leave me alone!" Olivia pushed her chair back and left the dining room. By the time she got to the stairs, I was right behind her, yelling at her to stop, while Henri was behind me, yelling at me to stop. We were all screaming at each other, and no one was listening. Olivia stomped up to her bedroom. Then, Henri went into the TV room, slamming the door behind him. The sound of it reverberated in my head as I walked to the empty kitchen. Standing at the sink, I stared at my reflection in the dark window, wondering what was happening to us.

I didn't sleep much those nights. Lying awake in bed for hours, watching the moon outside our window slowly drift across the night sky, I could sometimes hear the faint sound of coyotes in the distant hills. I imagined the coyotes coming for my daughter, like the Hounds from Hades. They'd wait for her to slip up, perhaps on nights after she'd forgotten to take a dose or two of her anti-depression meds. In my mind, the coyotes would silently circle under her window—tails down, their yellow eyes concentrated into slits as they listened, waiting to pounce on her. I could almost smell their damp fur.

One night, to convince myself she was okay, I slipped out of bed, crept across the floor so as not to wake Henri, and stood motionless at the bottom of the stairs. Even though it was past midnight on a school night, I heard Olivia sobbing in her room. I climbed the stairs, gently knocked on the door, and quietly pushed it forward. The faint hall light nudged her until she rolled over on her bed, still on top of the comforter, still fully dressed. She stopped crying for my benefit and tried to smile, but I couldn't help picturing a coyote hiding under her hoodie, biting and tearing at her skin until it bled.

"I'm fine, Mom. Go back to bed," she said. When I put my hand on her shoulder, her smile turned into a grimace as she let out a slow breath. "It hurts, Mommy. This pain hurts so much!"

Until then, I hadn't understood the chronic tension she felt, how the deep sorrow and anxiety of clinical depression attacks not only the mind but the body and soul as well. I was willing to do anything necessary to change my daughter's fate, but I needed more guidance.

Having secured a therapist for Olivia, I found one for myself, a Jungian scholar with a Ph.D. This woman was always impeccably dressed, as if she was about to fly off to give a talk at some conference—which she often did. She was short and had straight, dark hair. Sometimes, I couldn't take my eyes off the thin line of grey roots at the top of her head, wondering if mine looked any better.

Perched on the edge of her chair, she seemed owl-like. As I described Olivia's troubles, my therapist remained silent, rotating her head now and then or blinking as she asked a question. I imagined her dictating her notes after our sessions, building her case for my diagnosis. She was kind and patient with me, but I always felt she was holding something back, not revealing what she honestly thought.

Then, at one of our sessions, she slipped, or maybe she did this intentionally. Anyway, she gave me a hint. After listening to me talk yet again about my anxiety related to Olivia, she sat back, let out a sigh, and nodded. "You're just like Demeter."

"What do you mean?"

"You remember the ancient Greek myth about Demeter and Persephone?"

"Sort of. Remind me."

"Well, briefly, Persephone is a young goddess who goes looking for wildflowers one day, and Hades captures her. As she's screaming and crying, he drags her to the Underworld to be his wife."

"And? That's it?"

"No. Her mother, Demeter, goes crazy and roams the Earth, causing havoc in a desperate attempt to save Persephone."

"I can relate. What happens then?"

"You'll have to read the story."

But I didn't read the myth right away. I thought I knew all I needed to know. From my therapist's description, I already loved Demeter—every messy part of her. When I realized how dangerously depressed Olivia was, I, too, became a furious, frantic mother obsessed with rescuing my daughter. Demeter was my hero, a mother who was not about to let go.

———————

After months of intense work, Olivia's eating disorder seemed under control. She'd stopped binging and purging and was happier. By the time she started her junior year in high school, she'd joined a community crew team and had made some new friends. Still, I worried she might relapse. Convinced she needed me to ward off anything negative that might happen to her, I was always on alert. When she got a cold, I'd arrive in her room with decongestant medicine, Chinese herbs, Vicks VapoRub, and Gypsy Cold Care tea, then nag her to go to bed early every night so she wouldn't get sick again. If she were emotionally hurt, I'd try to mend her broken heart like I'd sew up a rip in her sweatshirt. I was anxious to make her world easier, incredulous that I'd allowed our daughter to be so miserable in the first place.

One night, as I was getting ready for bed, I stopped to look at the many family photos that lined a shelf in our bedroom—all frozen moments of innocence, carefully chosen, framed, and cherished. *What happened to that time in our lives?* I wondered. *Was it ever real? Was it stolen?* One picture caught my eye. It was an early fall day, the leaves in the background still mostly green. We were in a park with Henri's cousin, Janet, who'd wanted to take a photo of our family. Austin was around ten years old, and Olivia was six. Janet, who had us all laughing and groaning about having our picture taken, told us to cover our eyes and count to five. At three, we heard a click. The photo shows us smiling in anticipation, still covering our eyes with our hands, as instructed. It's as if we were playing a family game of hide-and-seek—all of us hiding, all of us wanting to be found.

"Come to bed," Henri said. I returned the photo to the shelf, turned off the light, and slid under the covers. A full moon was rising, washing the world in silvery silence. Reaching out, I found Henri's hand to hold. I needed to feel tethered.

"I never saw her depression coming," I said.

"You couldn't have known. None of us did."

"But I should have known. A mother is supposed to sense these things. We should have done something earlier."

"Like what? We did everything we could. This was going to happen no matter what we did. It's just the way things worked out."

"I'm not okay with that."

"Well, that's your problem, not mine."

"You can say that so easily?" I let go of his hand and rolled away. My mind short-circuited, then became as blank as the wall in front of me. I felt a slow tear work its way down the side of my nose.

After a long silence, Henri's voice startled me. "You know, I think you should go with your friends to Seville next month. They have everything planned. It would be good for you to get away for a while." I knew Henri was trying to be supportive. I also knew I would take this the wrong way.

"So, you think there's something wrong with me that a trip to Spain will fix?" My voice sounded a bit frantic, high-pitched, and too loud, like I was trying my best to balance on a tightrope while yelling to someone on the ground. "You think going away will solve something? Well, it won't. And anyway, how can I go? I can't leave Olivia now."

Henri turned toward me and gently hugged my shoulder, which was involuntarily jerking up and down. More tears threatened to roll down my cheeks, but I'd been taught well to hold them back. Plus, I didn't want the headache that always came after I cried. To me, letting go came with a price.

"She'll be fine for ten days. I'll be here, and she has her therapist," Henri said. "Going on a trip doesn't make you a bad mother." Just hearing the words "bad mother" was all it took. Without warning, a lone sob rose from deep within me, releasing a flood of tears. I cried until there was nothing left except my throbbing headache. Certainly, Olivia would be fine, I realized. It was me I was worried about. I didn't know how to leave.

The next day, I went to Austin's bedroom and found a book he had from high school on Greek mythology and turned to the *Homeric Hymn to Demeter*. I needed a mentor, a guide, a saint, a god. In my therapy sessions, I felt like I was just regurgitating my fears week after week rather than learning how to help Olivia. My mother was no use in this situation, and the self-help books I consumed left me feeling more guilty and ashamed. Taking the mythology book downstairs, I brewed a cup of tea and settled on the living room couch. A slate-grey haze shrouded the mountains. There were no birds flying, no squirrels running up and down the leafless trees. The world seemed despondent. As I began to read the myth, Demeter came to life in my mind.

DEMETER (RE-IMAGINED)
Her Daughter Lost

Demeter, Goddess of the Harvest, was nurturing and revered. Draped in long robes, her muscular shoulders bronzed by the sun, she smelled of rich soil and herbs—oregano, fennel, mint. Her role was to feed the people and animals by making the Earth green and the crops grow. Sometimes, she could even control the weather, forcing the wind to bring rain clouds to the fields.

One day, the god Zeus planted a seed deep in Demeter's fertile womb. Her body was like the Earth, and the child growing within became her world. From month to month, Demeter increased her responsibilities as a new mother. She ate only the best food and took long strolls in the early mornings. Placing her hands on her belly, she whispered sweet words to the presence inside. The baby expanded, claiming its space like a tiny shoot in the soil. First, it pressed against Demeter's stomach and liver, then pushed against her spine. With Demeter's skin stretched almost to the breaking point, the child finally burst into the sunlight.

Demeter lovingly nursed her daughter, Persephone, helping her learn to walk and teaching her all about the splendors of the Earth. Often described as "the one with the delicate ankles," Persephone grew to be a beautiful maiden—and her mother became increasingly protective of her. Demeter refused to let the young male gods come to call and only allowed Persephone to play in the fields if accompanied by other maidens. For the most part, Persephone obeyed. But she was also bright and curious, a spirited teenager unable to resist the heady temptations of youth when her mother wasn't looking.

While picking roses, crocus, and dreamy blue violets in the soft mead-

ow, Persephone wandered away from her friends, enticed by the narcotic fragrance of narcissus blooms, which had been planted to lure her. As she bent down to gather these flowers, the ground suddenly split open beneath her and the god Hades—bearded and fierce—grabbed her by the ankle, dragging her down the hole to be his bride in the Underworld. And then, she was gone.

When Demeter realized Persephone was missing, she became obsessed with finding her daughter. Day after day, she wouldn't eat, drink, or bathe. Like a crazy woman, Demeter first wailed and tore at her clothes, then wandered the land, dazed and frantic. In her mind, she could hear Persephone's screams resounding off the peaks of mountains and echoing into the depths of the sea.

Meeting Malvado

Henri was right. There was no reason for me not to go to Spain. My trip would be good for us all. I needed a break, and Olivia needed to know I was gaining confidence in her ability to handle stress. Plus, Spain had fascinated me since my high school years when I first came upon Hemingway's writings. So unlike Peoria, Seville was a place of tradition and mystery where bullfighters were local legends, and passionate flamenco dancers stomped their feet in dark taverns. I wanted to search for the hidden doors in monasteries where nuns were known to sell their famed pastries developed over centuries from Jewish, Muslim, and Catholic recipes. I also knew Seville was home to the Virgin of Hope of Macarena, Our Lady of Sorrows, the mother of all grieving mothers. I'd always loved Mary for some reason, maybe because I couldn't believe God was a man.

I packed what would fit in a carry-on bag: five interchangeable outfits, walking shoes, my journal, a small guidebook, and my camera. After landing in Madrid, I took another plane to Seville, then a taxi to our rented apartment.

"Hola! You're here!" Pilar swung open the apartment door, and Judy hugged me as I dragged myself inside. Located on the edge of a quiet neighborhood, the apartment was small with euro-clean lines and stark, modern furniture. In the white kitchen, I saw a table set with candles, delicacies from the local market, a loaf of fresh bread, and an opened bottle of red wine.

"I can't tell you how great it feels to be on vacation with you two," I said. "No husbands or jobs or children. Just us." The moment I spoke, a rush of heat rose from my chest and threatened to flood my eyes. Bending over, I hurried my bag into the bedroom, then emerged after a few minutes, smiling. I was determined to act normal and not dwell on Olivia. After dinner, we decided on our schedule for the following six days. Pilar and Judy would attend morning Spanish classes while I was free to roam the city alone. We agreed to meet for lunch and spend the afternoons and evenings together.

In the morning, I crossed the tree-lined park near our apartment and set out to explore Seville. I planned to visit churches to photograph the Virgin Mary. As I traveled through the city, I began noticing pictures of Mary painted high on the outside of church walls, not just inside. Hovering above the city's crowded avenues and side streets in her brilliant blue robes, she was never without that full-of-grace, all-knowing look in her eyes.

Walking down a narrow street, then twisting left at the corner, I came face-to-face with another image, an impish character drawn in pink spray paint on the side of an abandoned building. It was a small, cartoonish picture of a little girl. She had a circle for a head, a flip hairdo, a triangle body, two straight lines for legs. Another two lines, her arms, stuck out to either side. Standing straight and proud on this forgotten wall, she seemed unfazed by the Spanish and Arabic scribblings surrounding her. I decided to name her "Graffiti Girl." She was charming, like my own daughter. I took a picture to remember my delight at finding her, not realizing we would meet again.

The following day, I wandered through a different neighborhood, a tattered part of the city, where I was to meet my friends for lunch. To my surprise, Graffiti Girl was there, too, but this time, she was a new version of herself. She was a gigantic, yellow figure that filled a corrugated metal door. After lunch, taking a new route back to our apartment, I found her again—a tiny drawing this time, only a few inches high, sketched in sky-blue chalk on a brass handle.

For several days, I kept running into Graffiti Girl. I'd find her around a corner or at the end of a block. Amid the city's grit, her playful image danced within a canvas no higher than an upstretched hand might reach. She was a punctuation mark in the ongoing, run-on graffiti conversation that encircled Seville like the bottom of a fluttering flamenco skirt.

The more I encountered Graffiti Girl as I traversed the city, the more I noticed Mother Mary just above the line of urban scrawl. Like the story of Demeter and Persephone, I imagined Mary and her Spanish daughter, Graffiti Girl, living parallel lives in Seville, conscious of each other's existence but painfully separated, unable to connect.

On the last evening of our trip, after a deliciously fun dinner at a local taverna, Pilar, Judy, and I wove through Seville's streets toward our apartment. I looked everywhere for Graffiti Girl, hoping to snap a parting photo. At one point, we decided to take a shortcut down an alley. Aside from a lone, bald light hanging from a doorway, black shadows extended their reach onto the cobblestones.

I quickened my steps and kept my eyes down, watching for rodents that might dart between pails of souring garbage. When I looked up, I saw something strange. Dominating a dingy red door was a gigantic drawing of a man's bald head. With a cigarette protruding from one corner of his sneer and uncaring eyes drawn as two black lines, he looked like a pimp or a pusher.

Then, I saw her. I couldn't move, couldn't breathe. To the man's left was a small white image of Graffiti Girl looking innocent and unaware of his presence. I thought of Olivia and suddenly felt cold. Was this a premonition of some kind? A warning? A threat? I wanted to pull Graffiti Girl away from him, but there was nothing to grab. Instead, I took a photo.

In the morning, Judy, Pilar, and I boarded our plane to return to the States. Later, Judy said I cried all the way home on the plane, but I had no memory of it.

"Oh, come on," I said. "Maybe I was a little upset for a while. I felt like I'd just seen a ghost or something that last night."

"No, you were sobbing, hard, for a long time. Pilar and I were worried about you. Even the stewardess stopped to check on you."

"Well, I'm fine now," I said.

Still, for the next several weeks, the word "Malvado" kept surfacing in my mind—a Spanish name referring to someone malicious or evil. I couldn't stop thinking about the man from Spain. I didn't realize when I took the photo that he'd become a stowaway in my camera. He followed me home.

Tongue-Tied

Malvado didn't appear right away. He stayed in the shadows. Waiting to make his entrance, he was content to watch. I sensed something wasn't right, and each day, I slipped a little deeper into despair.

Toward the end of high school, when Olivia broke up with her boyfriend, she spiraled further down, too. Not only was her heart broken, so was her spirit. She quit the rowing team and gave up trying to prove herself to the smart, successful students. Instead, she found an even edgier group of friends—they took risks, they took drugs, they took her in. That summer, I watched her morph into someone tougher. She switched from wearing athletic shorts and Nike tops to baggy t-shirts and vintage baseball caps. Her music, speech, and ideas became cruder. And she had a defiant attitude.

"There's a clump of grass stuck to the bottom of the Prius. Where were you driving last night?" I asked her one day in August. I'd noticed grass stains on the bottom of her jeans, too.

"Oh, I went with friends to a field in the country. We wanted to look at the stars," she said.

"You told me you were going to the movies." Olivia let out a long sigh and stared at me. The air between us became taut.

"Well," she said slowly, tilting her head toward me, "we changed our minds." I tried to hold steady and return her glare but felt like I was standing in quicksand.

"Seems like you guys do a lot of partying lately," I said. "And you're often the one driving?"

"Yes, I drive us around. Okay?" Before I could say anything, she grabbed her bag from the kitchen counter and walked toward the screen door. "I'm late to meet someone now." I watched her push the door wide open, then waited to hear it slam.

"How am I supposed to deal with her?" I asked a friend over the phone.

"She's almost an adult," my friend said. "I figure my kid will do whatever she wants in a few months once she gets to college, so there's no point in giving her rules now." That didn't make sense to me, but I didn't argue. Instead, I waited. I was anxious for Olivia to get to college, to have a new focus, to find new friends. The summer months passed like molasses.

Olivia was excited about signing up for classes at the College of Charleston and being near the South Carolina coast. We allowed her to take a car to college if she agreed to attend regular sessions with a therapist and keep up her grades. At first, Olivia seemed happy, but by the second semester, her calls home almost always came attached to a crisis—one time, she lost her cell phone. Another time, someone stole her wallet at a dance. Too often, she reported forgetting to take her anti-depression medication and having trouble concentrating on homework. Uninterested in drunken frat parties, she preferred to hang out with "a more creative crowd." She also found a new boyfriend who'd dropped out of college at the beginning of the semester. Tyler played music and lived in a group house in a sketchy part of Charleston. Everything he did seemed exciting to Olivia.

By mid-fall of her sophomore year, Olivia rarely returned our phone calls. Henri and I decided to see what was going on with her and drove to Charleston for a weekend. We'd arranged to meet Olivia for dinner and go with her to a play on campus.

A few days before leaving for Charleston, I began practicing what I wanted to say to my daughter. I'd scribble thoughts in my journal, cross them out, start over. My intention was to voice my concerns without giving advice. This was something I'd been working on ever since the year I decided to give up giving advice for Lent.

I wasn't Catholic, and I'd never seriously tried to renounce anything for Lent, but sometimes I'd give it a shot. One year, I gave up chocolate (that lasted a week). Another time, it was gluten (that lasted a few days). Still, I was intrigued by the notion of letting go.

"Guess what I'm doing for Lent this year?" I asked. Olivia and Henri swapped glances. "I'm giving up giving advice." It was kind of a joke, and I thought they'd laugh. Instead, Olivia jumped up and hugged me. Henri smiled and nodded his head in approval. It seemed my advice was no longer needed or welcomed. I felt my cheeks flush.

"Wow! That's GREAT, Mom!"

"Well, not forever, you know," I said. "Just for Lent. And don't worry, I'll fill your basket on Easter Sunday with advice printed on little sticky notes." No one thought that was funny at all.

For two weeks, my tongue was swollen and bruised from me biting it whenever I wanted to add my two cents to a conversation. I felt like a nun who'd taken a vow of silence. After another week, my observation skills became sharper as I witnessed what triggered me. In the evenings, I'd notice myself squirming as Olivia watched a stupid TV show before dinner instead of tackling her homework. Or, on frigid mornings, when Olivia would bop downstairs on her way to school wearing only a thin shirt, skirt, and sneakers, I wouldn't say a word but would feel chilly and find a sweater to put on.

Sometimes, sitting alone in front of the fire after dinner, I wouldn't know what to do with myself. I felt invisible, useless. It was my first hint that perhaps my need to feel needed overshadowed the guidance I hoped to give my children. After Easter and the obligatory forty days of purification and self-denial, I revived my voice, but I'd been humbled. I tried my best to listen more and talk less.

For a while, this approach seemed to be working. Olivia started sharing songs with me from her playlist. I'd show her funny cartoons. We'd cook together in the kitchen and sing old Four Tops songs as we did the dishes. But after her first year of college, Olivia sank into another dark depression, and we started drifting apart again. I worried I might push her further away if we argued. I became tongue-tied, not wanting to give advice but not knowing what else to say. Eventually, my fear made me mute.

———

Henri and I arrived early at the restaurant in Charleston and found a table outside under a canopy lit with tiny white lights. A strong smell of garlic mixed with the sweet fragrance of low country blooms. Our waiter was a college student, buoyant and friendly. I'd hoped Olivia's boyfriend might be more like this kid.

A girl wearing a short black dress, grey hoodie, and stockings with a big run up one leg sauntered to our table and sat down. I hardly recognized my daughter. Her hair was dirty, she seemed pale and thin, and it looked like she hadn't brushed her teeth for days. As we waited for our order to be taken, Olivia couldn't sit still. Her knee was bouncing up and down, and she kept fidgeting with her hair, tossing it to one side or the other.

"What would you like to eat?" Henri asked, turning to Olivia.

"I'm not hungry. I ate something earlier, and my stomach kind of hurts now," Olivia said. She looked ready to cry. The three of us silently sipped our water. "This isn't the best time for you guys to be here," she said. "I don't feel well enough to go to the play tonight." Henri and I stared at her. Then, before we could say anything, Olivia stood up and laid her car keys on the table. "You might as well take my car home," she said. "My grades won't be good this semester. I got behind." She hugged us and walked out of the restaurant. That was the end of our visit.

The next day, we drove her car back to Asheville. I contacted Olivia's therapist in Charleston on Monday to discuss our concerns. She assured me they were working through things. Then, a month later, Olivia called me while I was driving to do some errands.

"Hi, Olivia!" I said when I picked up the phone. I was always happy to hear from my daughter—always hopeful things with her were better.

"I need to tell you something," Olivia said. "Tyler's going out West, and I want to go with him." Her voice sounded rushed, as if she wanted to get off the phone and not have this conversation at all.

"Out West is a big place. What's your plan?" I asked, stalling for time, my chest tightening. I pulled into a parking lot and stopped my car, unable to concentrate on the road.

"I don't know where we're going, Mom. Don't worry. We can figure it out."

"Well, we have an agreement. We said we'll support you if you go to college or do an internship, but not if you just want to hang out."

"I know. We'll get jobs and stuff."

"That's not much of a plan. So, in that case, I guess you realize you won't have a car or money from us. Have you thought through all this?"

Apparently, she hadn't, especially the part about not having a car. Of course, Tyler didn't have a car. Two weeks later, she convinced him to move to Asheville as an extended stopover on his way to California while she stayed in Charleston to finish her fall semester. He rented a room in an apartment and got a job at a fast-food place. She planned to transfer in January to UNC-Asheville and stay until she graduated. They both seemed willing to compromise and quite anxious to get out of Charleston.

That December, when Olivia arrived home for Christmas, I noticed her green army jacket was frayed at the bottom, and her jeans were dirty. The fitted sweater I bought her earlier in the fall now seemed voluminous. She had dark circles under her eyes, and her teeth were yellow. When she went to the dentist appointment we'd arranged, she had six cavities. I assumed her teeth had suffered while she was bulimic, but I hoped all that was in the past. I focused instead on how relieved she seemed to be back in Asheville. It felt good to have her home.

Olivia moved into an apartment near campus with a classmate. Henri and I tried to treat her as if she were away at college, not down the street. We didn't want to pry into her life, although we insisted that she get a therapist in town. By March, we could tell Olivia was struggling. What we didn't know was that she was getting high most nights, staying up late, oversleeping in the mornings—missing therapy appointments, missing classes, missing life.

At night, when it was just Henri and me, conversations always circled back to Olivia. We felt we had to stay one step ahead of her, but we had no idea how to do that.

"What is going on with her?" Henri asked one evening at dinner.

"I honestly don't know." I'd run out of ideas, suggestions, advice.

"Well, something's got to be done. We've tried everything—talking to her, getting her into therapy, taking away her car—but nothing works." Henri and I sat in silence for the rest of the meal. I got up to clear the dishes. He made another drink and went to watch TV. Evenings were like this, week after week, month after month.

In late May, one of Olivia's close friends from high school overdosed and died. This tragedy was difficult for everyone who knew him, but for Olivia, the pain was unmanageable. She cried, of course. She was also jittery, unable to calm down, and didn't want to talk to us. It was like she was on fire. Then, a few weeks later, she acted differently. When I picked her up on Father's Day to join us for brunch, she was slurring her words and telling me to chill out. I asked her if she was high, but she waved me off with an annoyed look, saying I was making things up. I knew then that I was losing her again.

Part Two

The Gulf Widens

Late that summer, Olivia asked if I would come to her next therapy appointment in Asheville. I was thrilled. Finally, we were getting somewhere. I didn't care if she was angry with me. I was willing to do whatever it took to work things out. When I arrived, a receptionist escorted me to the therapist's office.

The room was tiny, like a converted closet, with one small window that allowed little light or air. Olivia was already seated in a chair next to her therapist's desk. I sat on the miniature loveseat. The room was so tight that when the therapist swiveled around to face us, all our knees were practically touching. After a long silence, the therapist, who looked to be in her early thirties, nodded to Olivia.

"I just need to tell you something," Olivia said. "It's something that happened a while ago. Things are fine now."

"Alright."

Olivia took a deep breath. "When I was at College of Charleston, I got addicted to heroin." That was it. No gentle lead-up. Olivia wanted this to be out and over. For a moment, I could only stare at her, squeezing my hands farther into my lap. I noticed a voice in my head telling me to stay calm and listen, but that only made it harder to comprehend the words coming out of my daughter's mouth.

"When did this happen?" I asked.

"Last spring. Tyler and I thought we would try it, but once we started doing it all the time, I couldn't stop. That's why we decided to leave Charleston. We thought it would be better because back then, you couldn't find heroin in Asheville, not like in Charleston. It's easier to get it here now, but you don't need to worry. I'm not doing it anymore. I just wanted to tell you."

Olivia didn't say she needed help. What she said (rather matter-of-factly, as if explaining something to a child) was that she "got addicted," but that was in the past. No big deal, end of story. I tried to think of anything to ask her. I needed more information, more time.

"How did this happen?" I repeated, sounding thickheaded. The furniture in the tiny office started slowly growing, closing in on me. I was looking at Olivia, holding my breath.

"At first, heroin was great," Olivia said. "I mean really fantastic. You can't imagine how good it feels. I've tried lots of things, like cocaine and pills, but once I tried heroin, I wanted more right away. It made me feel normal and happy. I started snorting it, then using it every day, then shooting up." I slowly nodded my head, pretending I could handle what she was telling me when all I wanted to do was run out of the room before she could say anything more.

We were all very quiet. Olivia turned to stare out the window and let out a long sigh. By now, her bravado had vanished. I watched a tear roll down her cheek and rest on the bottom of her chin. Another slowly followed. With her head down, she spoke to the floor. Her voice was soft, small.

"After a while, I don't know." She sighed. "It was bad…it just became a job." The room was stifling. I sat on the edge of the loveseat, my gut balling into a tight knot, threatening to pitch whatever was in my stomach all over the therapist's lap. The voice in my head was screaming. *Say something! Don't let her leave the room. Don't let this be happening!* My legs and arms were quivering, but I forced myself to be calm, squeezing my hands tighter. Olivia and her therapist waited for my response.

I took in a slow breath and exhaled, suddenly feeling not angry or afraid but defeated. My body collapsed a bit, and I sank farther into the loveseat. Finally, I defaulted to the only words available: "Oh, Olivia. I am so sorry."

And I was. I was sorry things had gotten so bad for her, sorry she had been so foolish and reckless as to try heroin. I was sorry she had taken yet another wrong turn in her life and sorry I hadn't prevented it. I was sorry I didn't know what to say, sorry I would have to tell Henri, sorry I couldn't walk out of the room and not hear any of this.

"I was afraid, Mom. So, I asked a friend how to kick it. I did what he said, using another drug for a while, then eased off that. It was just before Christmas last year. I was at home."

"Last Christmas? What do you mean?"

"Yeah, you know, it was early in December when I came home after classes were over in Charleston. Remember? I was up in my room and told you I had the flu for a few days. That's what was happening. I was going through withdrawal in my bedroom. It was awful. But I don't do heroin anymore. I just do milder drugs, like weed. It's okay, Mom. I'm fine now."

I was still trying to listen, still struggling to keep my mouth closed, trying not to act as if I'd just been kicked in the teeth. I mumbled something like "thank-you-for-telling-me" and "you'll-have-to-tell-your-dad" and "I-don't-know-what-to-say" and "we'll-have-to-discuss-this-together-when-he's-back-in-town."

We all stood up. Olivia gave me a quick hug goodbye and left. The therapist hugged me, too, as if everything was fine now.

"I work with lots of kids who are in worse trouble than this," she said as she patted me on the back. I stared at her. *She's young. She has no children, at least none old enough to be adolescents. She has no idea.* Then, before I could say anything, she escorted me out her office and motioned for her next client to come in.

I don't remember walking across the parking lot and opening my car door. I just remember sitting in the driver's seat for a long time, mesmerized by two birds bouncing from branch to branch in a nearby bush, fluttering their wings as they worked on building a nest. How I wanted to be like them. Such a simple life. When one of them flew away, I was jolted back to my reality, felt the tears on my cheeks, and started the car.

It was late afternoon by the time I got home. I entered the kitchen, threw my keys on the counter, and sat on a stool. My breathing was shallow, and my chest felt tight, but my mind was numb, my thoughts jumbled. After a while, I realized I was rocking back and forth, staring at the floor in a daze. I stood up and started pacing around the kitchen—walking to the window, back to the sink, over to the living room, back to the window. I wasn't hungry but opened the refrigerator anyway and stood in its cold light. It was empty. I hadn't shopped for dinner because Henri was out of town. He'd gone on a kayak trip down the Grand Canyon with buddies and wouldn't be home for another ten days. I couldn't reach him. I was too terrified and shocked to do anything. My heart had not simply stopped, not like that time in the kitchen with Maria Callas. This time, a grenade had exploded inside my chest, leaving everything torn apart. I didn't know how I would survive. Even though the therapist seemed to think Olivia's problems were nothing to worry about, I knew better. This was not normal teenage behavior, even for Olivia. My Persephone had slipped under the Earth.

I kept looking out the window, watching the sun lower itself into an indifferent horizon. When our house grew darker, horrifying images became more vivid in my head: Olivia relapsing, accidentally overdosing in some public bathroom with a needle stuck in her arm, or getting high, crashing her car, and ending up alone and dead in a ditch.

"Jesus, Olivia! Heroin?" I yelled. "How did I not see THIS coming?"

I walked onto our deck, hoping for solace. When the black mountains offered nothing, I fiercely prayed to the empty, colorless sky. *Please don't let her die.* Then my eye caught a slight, red glow in the shadows at the far edge of the deck.

I only saw his silhouette, but I knew it was Malvado, the man from the back alley in Seville. He was sitting in the dark on one of our wooden porch chairs, a thin trail of smoke from his cigarette drifting up into the trees. A shiver ran through me. I wondered how he got there, what he wanted. Was he even there, or was my mind playing tricks? I couldn't be sure. I crept back into the house and pulled the heavy sliding glass door shut, hoping the sound of locking it would keep him outside.

The following Monday, I told my therapist everything that had happened with Olivia. Close to the end of our session, I admitted something else. "I'm not sure what's going on. I've been imagining that a man is stalking me. I know it's not real. It's just in my head. This started when I saw a drawing of him on a wall of graffiti in Spain."

"What happens when this man appears?"

"I start to shake or sweat. I feel nervous, like I'm doing something wrong. Am I losing it?"

"No, it's quite normal for people in trauma to have experiences like this. Having a child facing an eating disorder or drug addiction can cause repeated trauma or long-term PTSD for any parent. It's the mind's way of processing something threatening."

"What can I do?"

"Recognize it for what it is. This man is a sub-personality of yours that's out of balance. We have many characteristics within us. Most people have sub-personalities like "the pleaser," "the adventurer," or "the rebel." This man sounds like he represents your inner critic. He's all the voices of your mother, or society, or others who may judge you rolled into one character. He's your foil, but he doesn't have to always be in charge."

"So, when he appears, or when I imagine what he's thinking, how do I make him stop?"

"Ask him why he's there."

"I know the answer. He's there to remind me what a lousy job I'm doing as a mother. He always shows up when I feel like I've blown it with Olivia or don't know what to do."

"He feeds on your insecurities about the past or the future. So, try bringing in another part of you. A wise teacher, maybe. Someone you trust to tell you the truth about yourself or who can remind you to stay present. It helps to have a gesture, like putting your hand on your heart, as a signal for that other personality to step up."

"But I believe what he's saying."

"Then you have more work to do."

When I left therapy, I went home and wrote in my journal. It seemed like the best place for me to take on Malvado. If I could observe him, maybe he wouldn't ambush me so often. On the page, I could make him smaller and reduce the power of his judgments. I could even try adding supportive thoughts for myself. I wasn't ready to do what my therapist had suggested, but by writing about him, I found I could make him tangible again, like the drawing in Spain, instead of ghostlike.

DEMETER (RE-IMAGINED)
A Torch in Each Hand

Demeter traveled to the farthest corners of the world, searching for her daughter. In each hand, she carried a torch. Looking up from the Underworld through cracks in the Earth, Persephone could see flashes of light as her mother passed above ground.

"I'm down here!" Persephone would shout, but her mother couldn't hear her—she was deaf from anxiety.

Demeter kept searching for clues, demanding information, but no one was willing to tell her the truth about what had happened to Persephone. Finally, she decided to go to a seer, the Sun God Helios, the one with divine vision whose golden robes were blindingly bright. Demeter tried to act calm as she waited for him to speak, but she couldn't stop tapping her foot on the marble floor. When Helios revealed that Demeter's precious daughter was captured to be Queen of the Dead, it was as if he'd handed her a hot coal—smoldering, still red, burning her fingers.

"Being Hade's bride might not be such a bad thing," he said. It was known that Helios could see into the future, but Demeter was too distraught to hear his wisdom or ask what he meant.

Later, Demeter learned Zeus had allowed Hades to kidnap Persephone. Being outwitted unleashed Demeter's maternal fury—her anguish turned to wrath. Riding a chariot pulled by two dragons, she was a fearsome sight as she stormed off in search of Persephone. For days, Demeter refused to eat or drink. The only thing she cared about was rescuing her daughter.

Initiation

I knew next to nothing about addiction, let alone heroin. In 2013, newspapers were beginning to expose the opioid crisis in America. Drug overdoses nearly tripled from 1999 to 2014. My friends and I used to read these articles and shake our heads in dismay. Back then, heroin use still seemed like something that only happened in big cities, not in our local schools and colleges or among the people we knew.

I remembered a time when Henri and I went to a wedding for the daughter of a medical school friend of his. It was before Olivia left for college. At the reception, we'd met an interesting couple—he was a lawyer, she a doctor. We'd talked about our children.

"Our daughter and her boyfriend are in their thirties and living in our basement right now," the woman said. "They're both recovering heroin addicts and trying to find jobs." The conversation ended, but I kept thinking about it.

"It was so sad to hear that couple talk about their daughter," I'd said to Henri once we were in our hotel room. "They were so matter-of-fact about it. I can't imagine having a daughter who's a heroin addict. What a nightmare."

After my session with Olivia and her therapist, I wanted to call this couple, apologize for not knowing how they felt, tell them I was in the fire, too. I realized my friends would never understand how I was feeling. How could they? Then, I felt guilty, thinking of all the mothers with addicted children who didn't have partners, couldn't afford therapy, or were trapped in their own addictions. Given my level of privilege, I didn't feel I had the right to identify with their pain. The more isolated I felt, the more I shut down. For days, I stopped returning phone calls and couldn't listen to music. I wanted everything to be still, quiet, empty, so I wouldn't have to feel anything at all.

Once Henri returned from his trip, I told him Olivia needed to discuss something with us. We arranged to meet her at a nearby café. Henri was looking forward to seeing her. We arrived before Olivia and sat on elevated stools around a high, somewhat sticky table for four. I couldn't touch the ground with my feet, so I leaned on the table for support. The smell of coffee, usually enticing, was making me nauseous.

We watched through the window as our daughter drove up, parked her car, yanked on the heavy glass door, and walked toward our table. She was dressed like a typical college kid, wearing a short skirt and loose top, her thick curls wound and piled on top of her head. For a moment, I pretended everything was fine. She kissed us both, sat down, and looked at her dad.

"So, did Mom tell you?"

"She didn't tell me anything. What's up?"

Olivia sighed. "I already went through all this with her…but now, I need to tell you. When I was in Charleston at college, I was addicted to heroin, but I'm not anymore."

Before she could say another word, Henri leaned his head down onto the table, put his face in his hands, and sobbed. Like many men, Henri was not practiced at crying, so his sobs sounded more like gasps for air. Having lost his father when he was eight and his mother when he was twenty-nine, Henri usually only cried at funerals when he could stand in the back of the room. On rare occasions, when we watched a sad movie, I'd feel his shoulders shake next to me and see tears flowing freely. I'd offer him a tissue, but he never took one.

Olivia and I didn't know what to do. We both just stared at him, watching his shoulders move up and down. Then he looked up at her and blurted, "I don't want to lose you."

"I am so sorry, Daddy." Olivia took his hand, rubbing back and forth on his fingers. I realized it was the first time she'd seen her father cry.

"I don't think I can talk about this right now," Henri told her, straightening up. "I got in late last night, and I'm exhausted. But we'll all need to discuss this further, Olivia."

"I'm leaving today to go with Tyler to his parents' house in South Carolina for four days. Can we talk after that?"

"Yes, but don't call saying you can't make it home. This is serious."

Henri and I drove home in silence. It would take a while for this to sink in with him, I figured, just like it had for me. He immediately went to work in the garden, the place he always went to think, to regain himself. We made small talk over dinner. It wasn't until we were getting ready for bed that he finally spoke about Olivia.

"We failed her," he said.

"That might be true, but it doesn't help to focus on that right now. We've got to decide what to do next. This is bigger than we know how to handle. She could relapse."

"Well, what do you suggest?" His voice was tight, exasperated. I expected this. I sat on the bed and waited for the electricity in the room to settle back down.

"I think we need help from someone who understands addiction," I said. Henri didn't respond at first. He walked into the bathroom, returned to the bedroom, and began slowly taking off his clothes. When he finally spoke, he was no longer angry. He sounded hopeless.

"You've tried therapy before with her," he said.

"I'm talking about getting a couples' therapist who can help us with a strategy. We only have a few years before Olivia is out of college and on her own. We have some leverage now to help her."

"That's true, but therapy isn't the answer for everything, you know."

"It's important we stay united in helping her, or it won't work," I said. I could already see how it would go. Olivia might try to split us, or we'd get exasperated and angry at each other like we did when she was bulimic in high school. "I'm not willing to ruin our marriage over this, and it's too important not to try everything we can for her sake."

"Well, you figure that out." He was hurt and frightened but also ready to surrender. I told him I'd begin looking for a therapist in the morning, then added, "We have to agree on what to say to Olivia."

"What can we say?" Henri asked. "We can't exactly punish her for stopping something she did in the past or for being willing to tell us about it. She'll never open up to us again."

"I know. It won't be easy."

Once in bed, we lay side-by-side in the dark, holding hands and holding back tears. His hand was much bigger and rougher than mine but also tender and warm. Over the past year, holding hands in bed had become our signal—a wordless truce if we were fighting or a reminder that no matter how lost we might feel, we still had each other.

"We failed her," Henri said again, but it was a whisper this time. My heart tightened. I wanted to say something to erase that thought. Instead, I squeezed his hand and remained quiet. That's when my nightmares started.

Tracks

There was a girl. Call her Sarah because I don't remember her name. I only remember that I was in middle school and our parents were friends. She was a few years older, old enough to drive to high school. I knew the roads she took every day—down Prospect, over the railroad tracks, then right onto Knoxville Avenue, and straight to Richwoods High.

As a child, I used to love watching trains go by on those tracks while we waited in our family car. I would count the train cars. Sometimes fifty or sixty would pass by filled with coal or grain, and I'd always wave to the man in the red caboose, who usually waved back. Until the early 1960s, Peoria was the third-largest rail gateway in the Midwest, but by the end of that decade, train traffic through town was freight-only and rapidly dwindling. Parents taught their teenage drivers to slow down and look both ways at every single railroad crossing. You never knew when a train might be coming—a single light in the distance was its only warning. There were no crossing flashers, no automatic lowering gates. The train had the right of way, and drivers were responsible for themselves.

For me, trains were familiar and fun until the last morning Sarah drove to school. I remember it was a crisp, sunny October day with a bright blue sky. I bet she was excited to see her friends on the cheerleading squad. Maybe she was running a little late. Near the tracks, the police said they found the pile of glass and twisted red metal that once was Sarah's new Mustang. They said the radio kept blasting rock and roll as they tried to pry her smashed body from the wreckage. When I heard the news, I wanted to know what song was playing when she died. I knew that radio station, WLOS from Chicago—we all listened to it. Was it a

50

Beatles song? Maybe the Rolling Stones? Why didn't they tell us? Why couldn't I know?

When I finally got my driver's license, my mother told me, again and again, to watch out for trains at every crossing, among a long list of other warnings to keep me out of danger. After listening to her, I was so careful I never had a car accident or a speeding ticket. In high school, I was the designated driver for my friends who wanted to smoke and drink.

By the time I got to college, things had changed. My friends and I played loud music, took drugs, danced late into the night at Saturday parties, and studied only when we had to. We'd get stoned after dinner and go to the edge of a bluff behind the library to watch the sunset. On weekends, we went for walks in the country, often near a railroad bridge a short distance from campus. The bridge was lengthy and crossed over the Kokosing River, an Ohio tributary that eventually drained into the Mississippi, just like the Illinois River did back home. There were wide spaces between the wooden slats with little room on either side of the rails, which made it hard to run without tripping. Once, when I was brave enough to venture out to the middle of the bridge, I thought I heard a train whistle somewhere in the distance. My heart started pumping blood, getting my muscles ready to race for my life, but I couldn't commit to going left or right. Instead, I stood in the middle of the bridge and started to shake. My friends laughed at me because the train never came. None of them felt the same terror.

I tried to tell my teenage daughter to run when I saw her sitting, one late afternoon, on a railroad track, oblivious to an oncoming train, her earbuds attached to her iPhone, blasting music, just like Sarah. I tried to scream, but no sound came out of my mouth. I ran to tackle her, to throw her off track, but I wasn't fast enough. I bolted straight up in bed right before the train hit—panting, my eyes wide open. After Olivia told me about her addiction, I had this same dream again and again for months.

I constantly worried about Olivia when she was a freshman in college, even though my friends thought I was overreacting. I knew she was using marijuana, which seemed normal to me, but in conversations with her, I also learned some of her classmates had serious drug habits and had spent time in rehab. Other things concerned me, as well. Once, she told me Tyler expected her to give him rides home when his shift ended after midnight, even though she had early morning classes. Another time, she let it slip that she'd helped pay his rent. I was hoping she'd soon wise up, but I was the one who was unwise.

After Olivia told me about her heroin addiction, I rarely slept. I'd hear a distant train whistle and think about Sarah's mom, how she'd looked like a ghost at the funeral, as if a train had run over her, too. The sadness I'd seen in her eyes told me never to let something like that happen to my children. But I'd ignored all the warning signs, all the flashers.

It's easy for a mother to miss signals when her obsessive worrying becomes a daily habit. Fear creates chaos in her mind until she becomes immobilized. To combat feeling overwhelmed, she focuses on staying in control rather than using her maternal instincts to clearly assess a situation. Add society's emphasis on blaming and shaming mothers for not being perfect, and all she's left with is her anxiety about being a failure. I was just beginning to understand this disconnect, my lack of faith in myself.

One night, I had a different dream about a train. This time, there was a car parked on the tracks. As the train came thundering toward the parked car, I got there just in time. With Herculean maternal strength only possible in a dream, I pushed the car off the track just before the giant brute of a train flew by—its horn blaring, wheels squealing against the rails, the smell of diesel fouling the air. I let out a deep sigh. I'd finally saved my daughter from this monster. But when I looked inside, it wasn't Olivia sitting in the driver's seat. It was me.

A False Bottom

Before Henri and I had time to meet with a couples' therapist, Olivia solved our problem. She was still at Tyler's parents' house in South Carolina when the landline in our house rang. I picked up the phone and heard an official-sounding woman speak in a recorded voice: "This is the Aiken County Correctional Facility. Will you accept a call from…" Then I heard another recorded voice—a squeaky little girl's—say, "Olivia."

I thought it was a prank call or maybe a scam by some inmate who happened to be named Olivia and was trying to get money for bail. I hesitated and was about to hang up, then I thought again and said yes. There was a click.

"Olivia?"

"Hi, Mom. Could you give me Tyler's mom's number?" Her voice sounded breezy but also rushed.

"Wait, why are you calling from a correctional facility in South Carolina?"

"Oh. Well, I just need to call her to tell Tyler where I am. I got arrested for shoplift—" Then, *click*. I stared at the phone in my hand then put it to my ear again, expecting to hear my daughter speak, but the line was dead. That was her allotted twenty-second call from jail. A sour taste slipped under my tongue and stayed there. It was 4:30 in the afternoon. Offices would be closing soon. I didn't have time to call Henri. Plus, I knew he'd be slammed at work and unable to help.

When I looked around the living room, everything I saw—the modern white sofa, the high beige-colored walls, our streamlined kitchen—seemed useless. My world was too clean, too open, too orderly. There were no reference points for jail. All I could think of were Hollywood prison scenes: huge rows of cells with sliding metal doors, stinking medieval dungeons, or an Old West sheriff's office.

I sat down at the computer, fingers shaking. *Maybe the correctional facility has a number to call,* I thought, *like a customer service line for mothers who have no fucking idea how to deal with this.* Combing through the site with its infuriatingly long list of rules and regulations, I came to a section that explained Olivia needed to post bail to be released. The website noted a bail bond company conveniently located across the street from the correctional facility. "How thoughtful," I muttered to myself. When I called that number, a woman answered the phone.

"Oh, thank God you are not a recording!" I blurted. "I have a problem. My daughter's in jail." I said this as if it was the most impossible thing that could have ever happened in the world.

"Yes," the woman said.

"Well, I don't know what to do. What is the next step here?"

"You mean, how does she get out of jail?"

"Well, yes. She's never been in jail before. Neither have I." I realized I sounded ridiculous, but the woman took pity on me. She was kind and patient. I figured she was a mother, too.

"There's no way to get a message to your daughter. She will have to spend the night in jail. But if you wire money to the bond office, her name will be put on a list of inmates to be released after the hearing." I froze for a moment when she said the word "inmates," then stammered a thank you.

After wiring the money for bail, I found a number for the sheriff's office. The sheriff sounded bored but seemed to perk up when I told him my daughter desperately needed her medication. He grudgingly agreed to tell Olivia, once she was released, to walk to the bail bond office and call me. There was nothing more I could do.

Even though my first impulse was to jump in my car and drive three hours to South Carolina to greet Olivia when she got out of jail, I decided not to. I was pissed. *How could she be so stupid? I am not going to rescue her this time or make excuses. I've had enough!* We would pay her bail, and she could pay us back. After that, it would be up to her to figure out how to retrieve her impounded car from the police, drive home, and start her life over if she wanted our support.

Slowly, I pushed opened the heavy glass doors of the dining room, stepped onto the deck, and let out a long, deep roar. I hoped the mountains would echo my frustration all the way to Olivia in that jail in South Carolina. Then, I called Tyler's mother to tell her my daughter, the one I raised to know right from wrong, had been arrested for stealing.

"We wondered where Olivia was," Tyler's mom said. "We waited all day to hear from her. Let me talk to Tyler."

Later that day, I called her again. She said Tyler confessed that when he and Olivia went to Walmart, he told her to put bottles of vitamins, some CDs, and other things in her purse to steal. He waited to go through the checkout line with a few items but instructed her to walk straight to the car. When Tyler got to the parking lot, Olivia's locked car was there, but she was gone. He assumed a security man followed her outside and contacted the police. Since he didn't want to go to jail, too, Tyler called his dad to pick him up and pretended to have no idea where Olivia might be.

"Olivia will appear before the judge at 10 a.m. tomorrow," I told her.

"Don't worry," she said, "we'll go to the courthouse in the morning." Although I'd never met this woman, Olivia liked her. I didn't trust Tyler to take responsibility for his actions, but I was relieved that his mother agreed to intervene. Despite believing I was doing the right thing, I still felt guilty about not showing up. The following afternoon, I called Tyler's mother again to see what had happened at the courthouse.

"I got busy and lost track of the time. I didn't make it," she said.

"What about Tyler?"

"Tyler said he didn't sleep well and felt ill, so he didn't go, either." I felt sick to my stomach, got off the phone, and spewed curse words all over my kitchen. Malvado was loving this.

Olivia later told me she'd entered the courtroom in line with other female inmates, all wearing blue prison jumpsuits and leg chains. Looking out toward the people who'd come to watch, she saw no one there for her. The judge briefly heard Olivia's case, then dismissed her to be ushered back to the correctional facility without further explanation. Olivia said she'd assumed Henri and I had left her there to rot since that's exactly what her cellmate's mother had done.

There are pivotal moments in a life that, when seized, can change everything. A profound shift occurs, and nothing is ever the same. It may come in the form of a breakthrough or epiphany, a tragedy or miracle. I assumed going to jail would be one of those moments for Olivia. It wasn't.

Olivia tried to convince us that going to jail had been a wake-up call for her. After many contrite and tearful conversations, she promised to straighten up. Two months later, she got arrested again—this time, she and Tyler were eating at a Whole Foods deli counter and tried to leave without paying. Her friends convinced her that this was a minor offense and not to worry about it. Drug use had damaged her brain's ability to use proper judgment. Even though she was no longer using heroin, she was still lying, stealing, and manipulating her way through each day to get high on alcohol, pills, or marijuana.

If Olivia going to jail wasn't enough to "snap her out" of her addiction, it certainly woke me up. I realized there was no point in cajoling or consoling her anymore. Now, I was steaming mad at her. There was no point in trying to get through to someone in active addiction. However, I needed to set boundaries around the behaviors that I would no longer tolerate. When thoughts of doubt and shame started brewing in my head, I realized it was Malvado hoping to sabotage my resolve. An image of his bald head drawn on that backstreet in Spain came into focus, but I managed to shove it aside. I was sick of his judgments and tired of trying to be a perfect mother. Instead, I decided to trust my intuition—and get more help.

Henri and I talked with our therapist about the consequences we'd need to enforce for our daughter. I also found an addiction counselor for Olivia, Dr. Susan Holman. She was an internist, not a talk therapist, and had been the medical advisor for a drug treatment inpatient program near Asheville. After a few intake interviews, she only met with Olivia for half an hour every week to have her pee in a cup and check in. But this woman was different from all the other therapists Olivia had seen. Dr. Holman was a long-term recovering alcoholic, and for the first time, Olivia seemed to pay attention. Finally, here was someone who got it, not from a textbook but from personal experience. Dr. Holman knew what Olivia must do if she ever hoped to recover.

After their first session, Dr. Holman sent Olivia home with a video to share with us that explained addiction as a disease. For well-educated people, including Henri, a doctor, we were shocked at how poorly informed we were. New studies in brain science were starting to clarify the roles neurochemical imbalances and genetic pre-disposition play for people suffering from addiction. This helped make sense as to why, given all the college students who abuse and experiment with drugs and alcohol over four years, only a small number of them become seriously addicted. In 2013, connections between drug addiction and depression were just beginning to be discussed as a dual diagnosis in medical journals. Only a few rehab centers assumed that eating disorders, drug and alcohol addiction, gambling, and other types of addiction all had similar roots.

Olivia returned for her second visit with Dr. Holman with a page full of questions. As with diabetes or celiac disease, she learned there were logical reasons why her mind and body reacted differently to stimuli than most people. She was fascinated with deciphering which thoughts and behaviors were common to people suffering from addiction.

Dr. Holman told her that reading about addiction was not enough. She insisted that Olivia attend daily AA meetings and ignored her excuses about classes and homework. Dr. Holman wasn't interested in any of my excuses either.

"You and Henri need to listen carefully to everything your couple's therapist has to say," she told me over the phone. "If we're lucky, Olivia will fail at some point and realize she needs more help."

"What do you mean 'fail?' She might relapse or overdose by failing."

"Let's hope it doesn't come to that, but yes, she could. You can't force someone to want to recover. It must be their decision, and the easier you make it for them to avoid the hard work, the longer it will take for them to see for themselves that things have to change."

Dr. Holman told me about a family she'd worked with who had to lock their daughter out of the house at night. "It was in the middle of winter. She was freezing and had nowhere to sleep, but she got the message."

"I can't imagine doing that," I said.

"It wasn't easy, but for them, it was necessary."

When I asked how I was supposed to help Olivia, Dr. Holman told me to focus on my own program (whatever that meant) and got off the phone. I didn't appreciate her brusque approach. Hadn't I worked hard to get Olivia the help she needed all these years? And didn't I deserve any credit for finding Dr. Holman in the first place? From what I could tell, Dr. Holman was not impressed. She had little patience for parents and wasn't about to hold my hand through this.

I dutifully began attending Al-Anon. Every Thursday evening at a Presbyterian church in West Asheville, I went to a meeting for parents whose children were dealing with addiction. The first night I walked into the musty basement of that church, I wondered if I would have anything in common with the people there. Then, across the room, I recognized an old friend. Our eyes locked, but she said nothing. Instead, she stood up, walked over to hug me, then went back to her seat. I forced myself not to cry or turn around and leave the room. I didn't want a hug and didn't want to belong to this group. Now, someone knew that our family had a problem, that my daughter was an addict. I didn't want this to be happening. I figured I'd stay long enough to hear what they had to say, learn how to help Olivia, and be done with it.

A father, whose teenage son had just been arrested, read a tedious list of rules, then introduced a topic for discussion. Each group member sitting around the long wooden table was given a chance to share their thoughts or pass. I stayed quiet, trying not to look at anyone.

Most of the stories here are much worse than mine, I smugly noted. Still, I was worried.

At the end of the meeting, we all stood up, held hands, and said the serenity prayer—something about accepting what we cannot control. The leader encouraged everyone to "keep coming back." As we filed toward the door, several parents were laughing, smiling, or hugging each other. I hunched on my coat, kept my head down, and walked quickly through the dark parking lot to my car. I hadn't laughed in a long time, I realized, and I didn't sing anymore. I wanted what they had but didn't have the faintest idea how to get it.

Although Al-Anon stressed that parents "didn't cause" and "can't cure" addiction, I wasn't so sure. Whenever I worried aloud to friends that I might be to blame for Olivia's problems, they were quick to be supportive. "You did the best you could do," they'd say. This only made me furious. To me, that line always sounded like a cheap attempt to wipe away parental sins. At least if I was partially to blame, I reasoned, I was also powerful enough to save her.

My need for my daughter to get better followed me like a vapor. It hid in my bed and seeped into my clothes, weighing me down under a sea of sadness. Now and then, I'd catch the sweet scent of hope before it vanished, but mostly the vapor was putrid. Sometimes, it smelled sharp and rancid, like the time a mouse died in our wall behind the TV. Sometimes, it was sour or stale, like rotting food, a reminder of my daughter's gradual decline. I was always on edge because I knew I was smelling death. At any moment, Olivia could overdose. She could die.

Olivia was still in college and attending AA meetings, but I could tell she was fragile and struggling. Every time she went into a tailspin on the phone with me, I rode it right along with her. I was not detached or immune to emotional entanglements with my child the way our Al-Anon leaders encouraged us to be. I was not clean. I had a burning desire to play a significant role in saving her. I wanted redemption for my failure to protect her, and I would stop at nothing until I satisfied those cravings. More than simply obsessing about my daughter's recovery, I became addicted to it.

Henri supported my attending Al-Anon meetings, but he chose not to go. As the weeks wore on that fall, he became more withdrawn and irritable, tired that every conversation between us circled back to what was eating me alive. Because we were agitated in different ways, I felt alone in my attempts to rescue our daughter. Even after I'd read books on addiction and codependence, even after going to Al-Anon meetings where people talked about the importance of letting go, I still didn't believe anyone could appreciate what I was going through, not even my husband.

My daughter was a brilliant soul. She was creative and talented, smart and intuitive, charming and funny. She had a loving family and a comfortable life. Everything seemed okay. So, why couldn't she be more like me? Why did she behave so recklessly?

I'd always assumed I'd be able to understand my teenager. I'd been young once. When I was in college, I may not have been wild, but I also wasn't tame.

Into the Abyss

One weekend in college, I decided to go skydiving, hoping to impress a new boyfriend. My parents had no idea I was about to jump out of an airplane. There were no cell phones in the early '70s, and parents didn't hover. There was an unspoken agreement that kids could do whatever they wanted as long as they were smart enough not to get in trouble.

My boyfriend, his roommate, and I drove deep into the Midwest countryside past crisp just-harvested cornfields. Cows with nothing else to do watched us as we drove by. This was honest country, we thought, more real than our suburban homes. Even the heavy scent of manure was enticing to us. Eventually, we pulled into a parking lot, inhaled the last of our cigarettes, and strutted across the landing strip to a makeshift office.

Four guys who owned a Cessna twin-engine plane ran the skydiving school. Back then, no one skydived with you, and there was no microphone in a helmet with someone telling you what to do. Once you jumped, your life was in your own hands. Our instructor, a young muscle-bound guy in his late twenties, had been a pilot a few years earlier in Vietnam.

"Beginning skydivers often can't think clearly," he said, "so you will be attached to the plane with a long static line. When you reach the end of the line, the weight of your body will pull out the pins, and your chute will open." He didn't smile or reassure us but barked instructions like a drill sergeant. I started wondering if anyone would mind if I just stayed on the ground. "After you jump, extend your arms to each side and count slowly to three, like this: one thousand one, one thousand two… You'll need to pull your emergency chute cord if you get to six. Otherwise, you'll have about ten seconds before you hit the ground."

My boyfriend and I locked eyes for a moment.

"The emergency chute will be attached to your stomach," our instructor continued. "So, when you land, you might break your back, but you'll probably survive." At this point, I could feel my legs shaking, the tremor rising to my chest.

I don't need to impress anyone, I thought. *Why am I doing this?* Wearing a stiff canvas jumpsuit and heavy pack, I waddled to the tiny plane, trying to look confident. Once aboard, I was surprised there were no passenger seats. Instead, we sat on the metal floor next to a door that remained open. We took off, climbing up and into the sky, while the trees, cars, and houses below shrank to toy size. Thin clouds drifted below us. My stomach rose into my throat. The deafening engine noise made it impossible to hear anyone speak, so our instructor simply motioned when it was time for one of us to jump. My boyfriend volunteered. Sitting at the door, dangling his legs in the air, he looked like a little boy. Glancing back at me, he smiled, shrugged his shoulders, then jumped. One moment he was sitting at the door, then all I saw was blue sky. Next, it was his roommate's turn to disappear. I was last.

My entire body was shaking. I wanted to beg the pilot to turn around, but I dutifully inched my way to sit at the edge of the plane's open door. As instructed, I reached out to grip the strut above me with both hands and placed my left foot on the wheel rattling below. I was now completely out of the plane, my right foot dangling in the air. The wind was surprisingly strong. I felt like a bug clinging to a windshield going sixty miles an hour down the highway. Finally, when we passed over the target, the instructor hit me on my ass, the signal for me to let go and push away from the plane.

During our orientation, the instructor explained that we'd be free-falling to the ground at roughly 120 miles an hour for about three seconds, then the chute would open. But mine didn't. I counted "one thousand one, one thousand two, one thousand three." Then, "one thousand four, one thousand five…" I was spinning out of control, whipping around in the air like a flag in a tornado. I couldn't tell the sky from the ground and wondered if something had gone terribly wrong. *Did I count too fast? Should I pull the emergency chute? Should I start counting again?* I started again: "One thousand one, one thousand two…" I didn't realize

I was dangling from the static line, still attached instead of freed from the plane. The instructor saw what was happening and gave the line a mighty jerk so my chute would open. We had passed the target for my jump, but I didn't know that.

Once the merciless engine roar and smell of burning fuel flew away with the plane, I checked that the chute above my head wasn't torn and began my tranquil descent through space. Birds soared above and below me. The flat countryside expanded for miles in every direction. From my vantage point, the Earth looked like it was bending with possibilities over the horizon. I was so happy I started kicking my feet and singing an Allman Brothers song: "You're my blue skies, you're my sunny days…"

Startled from my reverie, I heard someone yelling on a megaphone from the ground. "Watch out! You're coming down over a four-lane highway!" Looking between my feet, I saw cars zooming directly below me. I was coming down fast. I knew to fix my eyes on the horizon rather than become paralyzed watching the ground rush up to meet me. I pulled one cord hard to the left and managed to land in a cornfield next to the highway. My instructor came running to help gather my chute, then we tromped back through the empty cornfield toward his car.

"Are you okay?" he asked. "You did everything right, but you gave me quite a scare."

"What happened?"

"I don't know. Probably somebody packed your chute wrong," he said and slid into the driver's seat. "Maybe it was meant for someone who weighed more than you." I stood by the car for a moment, feeling the blood drain from my face, hoping I wouldn't faint. As much as I loved the exhilarating feeling of floating through space, I decided to never jump from an airplane again.

Although I dabbled in danger, I knew to stay within limits. I thought Olivia would be the same way. I didn't realize how depression had taken control of her life. It was as if she'd pulled out of the driveway one day and never returned. She got high and drove to parties, drove to friends' houses, drove to concerts. Eventually, she drove over sidewalk curbs and signposts and into other cars. She drove to dark parts of town and made back-alley deals. She drove to steal stuff from Walmart. She drove us crazy and drove her life into the ground.

For me to tell Olivia to play it safe was like expecting the ocean to stop making waves. She'd allowed her self-medication for depression to morph from drinking at parties and smoking marijuana after school to a full-blown heroin addiction. Not only had she slipped through the cracks—the person we tried to reason with was no longer our daughter.

Free-falling and ill-equipped to handle so monstrous a catastrophe by myself, I spent hours reading and researching. When my therapist didn't seem to offer many answers, I turned to psychic energy workers and intuitive coaches for help. I was willing to try anything not to be blindsided again by my daughter's addictive thinking and behavior. And I would not give up.

I was Demeter, readying myself again and again for battle. I became all the mothers who pushed back when they were told to relax, the mothers who stubbornly persisted when they were shamed for getting too involved in their child's well-being. Demeter embodied something my generation was missing—she wasn't trying to be a perfect mom. Instead, she let her passion and indignation ignite her fury. Hers was a vindicating tale for every woman willing to go against all odds to rescue her child. Finally, I had a role model I could champion.

How Do I Know Thee?

It was an early November weekend. Dry leaves were already covering our yard, and the air had turned from chilly to cold. Olivia attended classes at the university and went to AA meetings every day. She also had weekly sessions with Dr. Holman. On weekends, Olivia often joined us for a family dinner at our house. We didn't invite Tyler. Henri and I decided that if she wanted to see him, we couldn't stop her, but we would have nothing to do with him. One Sunday evening, after we'd finished our ice cream, Henri, Olivia, and I sat in the living room to have tea around the fire.

"I found a rehab place for Tyler in Florida last week," Olivia said. "I convinced his parents they needed to find the money to send him. Then, I drove him to the airport."

"That's amazing, Olivia," Henri said.

"I'm so impressed you did that. He needs help," I said.

"Mom, you can't blame Tyler for everything that happened with me. If it wasn't him, it would have been someone else." She took a long sip of her tea. The fire snapped and crackled. "I need to go, too," she said. Henri and I looked at each other. Then Henri got up to put another log on the fire. "Dr. Holman suggested I spend a month in rehab over Christmas break. I could leave right after exams in early December and return to college in January."

We didn't talk about it anymore that evening, but I called Dr. Holman the next day.

"Do you think this is necessary?" I asked her. "Olivia attends AA meetings regularly and seems better now." I was still in denial that my daughter's addiction issues were severe.

"She may seem better, but she has a long way to go," said Dr. Holman. "Plus, I spoke with her lawyer, and he thinks spending a month in treatment will help expunge her shoplifting case."

Henri agreed that Olivia needed more help. Later that week, we called Austin to let him know the plan for his sister. He thought it was a good idea, too. I outwardly praised my daughter's courage, but I thought going to rehab seemed extreme. I couldn't imagine not having her home. I'd never celebrated Christmas without Henri and both our children. Plus, Christmas was my favorite holiday, perhaps because I'd gone away to boarding school and only came home a few times a year. It was the one time of year my parents, two older brothers, and I came together as a family.

While Austin and Olivia were growing up, I insisted we not travel over Christmas but establish our family traditions at home. I wanted our children to remember making cookies together and listening to Handel's *Messiah* while decorating the tree. And we always invited close friends over on Christmas Eve to share a candlelight dinner, sing carols, and play charades. Now, we'd be missing Olivia because of a cruel affliction she had to face alone.

Dr. Holman helped us identify a rehab facility in Tennessee that specialized in the dual diagnosis of depression and addiction. I called her to confirm the details of our arrangement.

"So, you think she can get her arrest record erased if she goes there for a month?" I asked.

"Hopefully Olivia will stay longer," Dr. Holman said.

"What do you mean?" The muscles in my back began to tighten as I fastened my maternal armor. I was hearing but no longer listening.

"The best case would be if Olivia didn't come home at all."

"I doubt that will happen. She'll want to come home. We can work out something with an outpatient program in town so she can finish college."

"We'll see."

I rarely get headaches, but after I hung up the phone, my brain felt as if I had a knife stuck in it. Any other illness allows parents to care for, comfort, and even dote on their child. I was willing to sacrifice not having my nineteen-year-old daughter home for Christmas if that could resolve her legal problems. Now, this counselor was telling me she might never come home again. I worried my daughter might be taken away forever. I didn't realize she'd already left.

––––––––––––

The day after Olivia's exams, we agreed to take her to rehab. The car was packed and running, our steaming coffee cups in their holders, but I wasn't ready. Stalling for more time, I went back into the house with the pretense of making sure nothing was forgotten. Upstairs on Olivia's bed was a letter explaining what she could and could not bring to rehab. I remembered helping her pack for summer camp. And later, when she was first going away to college, we laughed together as she tried to stuff too many things into her suitcase. But this wasn't college, and it wasn't camp.

I picked up an old high school notebook lying spread-eagled on the floor. In the front was a week's worth of neat class notes, followed by page after page of doodles, then nothing but empty white sheets. In her closet hung skirts too tight and blouses too low next to a pale blue robe with a brown cigarette hole burned through the hem. Under her bed, I found tiny black lace underwear and a single shoe that was scuffed and worn down. Olivia was always hard on her clothes and hard on herself.

Who is this girl? I wondered.

There's a quote I always loved from Anais Nin's journal where she wrote that love begins "where the myth fails. Then we love a human being, not our dream, but a human being with flaws." Standing in the middle of Olivia's bedroom before we drove her to rehab, I tried to remember. *When did I start truly loving my daughter and not my idea of who I thought she should be?*

Even before she was born, Olivia was a mystery to me, but an enchanting one. In the middle of my pregnancy with Olivia, I dreamt about her. Not a dream, exactly. It was more like a vision. I was drifting in and out of consciousness around 3 a.m. when I sensed someone standing next to my side of our bed, like a young child or our dog. But when I opened my eyes, I saw only empty space. Across the dim, moonless room, I saw the figure of a young girl standing in the doorway. She wore an old-fashioned white dress, lacy and long. It reminded me of a photograph I'd framed of my grandmother when she was eight years old.

The little girl in the doorway just stood there, her thick, dark curls almost touching her waist. I sat up in bed and rubbed my eyes—thinking how ridiculous it is to rub your eyes when you can't make sense of what you're seeing. Rubbing doesn't improve vision, but it gives your hands something to do while your brain tries to sort out what is unbelievable. I told myself I was seeing things or dreaming, and that the vision would be gone when I opened my eyes, but the little girl remained at the door.

After what seemed like a long time, she stomped her foot and said, quite defiantly, "I WANT to be here!" I saw her speak and heard her in my head, but, in fact, she made no noise my ears could register—it was as if I felt her saying this. Then, she vanished.

My first thought was that this old-fashioned girl was the spirit of my daughter still in the womb, and that I'd been given a glimpse of her formidable personality. I felt frightened but challenged. Sinking back onto my pillow, holding my belly, I might have even let a tiny, knowing smile slip between my lips. I loved the idea that my daughter would be tough, strong, a firecracker.

Much as I felt intimately connected to my daughter at that moment, I mistakenly thought I would intuitively always know her. I was her mother, after all. I didn't understand that the mother-daughter dance constantly needs updating. There are always new steps to learn. My mother didn't know how to teach me these skills because her mother never taught her. And so, hurt feelings were left unexplored, and many ruptures went unmended.

Henri insisted I invite my mother to come to Asheville for Olivia's birth. I told him it wasn't a good idea.

"What do you mean? Of course, your mother will want to be here."

"You don't understand my family. I don't want to call her."

"I think you're making a mistake. Just ask her."

So, I did. I took a deep breath, rang my parents' home number in Florida, and asked my mother if she'd like to come for the birth of her granddaughter.

"Well, if you really need me," she said.

"It's not so much that I need you, Mom, but I would love for you to be here. I am due to deliver on April 26. You could fly up for a few days."

"I'm not sure what I would do, and I don't think your father wants to come to Asheville before the golf season here is over. Why don't we just see you in June." The tone in her voice told me the conversation was over. There was no point in talking further. We said goodbye. I heard a click, waited a beat, then felt the door to my heart slam shut as I hung up the phone. Hot tears formed behind my eyes. I was furious—but not at my mother. I was angry with myself for letting my guard down.

My parents loved me dearly but didn't always know how to show it. They'd lived through the hardships of the Great Depression and the horrors of World War II. Once life normalized in the 1950s, they wanted their children to be independent and fit to survive. There was so little coddling in my family that it bordered on neglect.

In 1967, my father decided it would "be best" if I went to boarding school in New York, nearly one thousand miles away from home. This decision coincided with my father's desire to winter in Florida without worrying about raising a teenager. Plus, he figured, this would help groom me to find a successful Wall Street husband. I'd never heard of boarding school. None of my friends went away to a private high school. But I wanted to please him, so I said yes.

Dad was a man's man, only interested in business and sports. He never had sisters and felt threatened by the Women's Movement that was brewing in the 1960s. My mother was the classic 1950s wife. She was talented and smart, but she was afraid to make a move without her husband's approval. I hoped to be like my father, not my mom, so I did what I could to impress him. I would be strong and independent if that's what he wanted.

On the first day of boarding school, my parents dropped me off at my dorm. They only returned to attend my graduation. During those four years, I joined the Glee Club and became president of a folk music band. We gave multiple concerts each year, and I often sang solos. One year, our Glee Club worked hard to learn Stravinsky's *Symphony of Psalms*, performing the challenging piece in Manhattan with a boys' school chorus and full orchestra. Even though my parents went to all my brother's football games throughout high school and college (both home and away), they never came to hear me sing.

In my first year away from home, I broke my leg skiing and landed in Yonkers General Hospital for a week. I'd never been in a hospital. My friends at school were not old enough to drive, so they didn't come to visit. Only Mrs. Hurry, my dorm mother, showed up one day to drop off her famous shortbread cookies. Because I was a kid, the doctors didn't bother explaining why it was taking days to put me in a cast.

A teenage girl on my floor seemed to have been in the hospital forever—she knew all the nurses and hobbled around on crutches visiting new patients. Her right leg was amputated from the knee down. When I asked how that happened, she said she broke it in gym class, then it got infected, and gangrene set in.

Maybe I'll lose a leg and never leave, too, I thought. I had to get out of there. But when I talked to my parents on the phone, I told them I was fine. They sounded relieved and decided they didn't need to come to see me in the hospital. Although I didn't allow myself to acknowledge my disappointment, I remember thinking that if I ever had kids, I would show up for them.

DEMETER (RE-IMAGINED)
A Dark Place

Demeter knew how it felt to be captured and kept in a dark place. Once, her father, King Kronos, had imprisoned her. Kronos was a powerful god but lived in fear of a prophecy that his children would eventually overthrow him. To make sure that didn't occur, every time his wife, Rhea, gave birth, he would swallow the child. This happened with five of their children: Hestia, Demeter, Hera, Hades, and Poseidon. Devoured by the one man who was supposed to cherish and protect her, Demeter spent year after year imprisoned in the dark, acrid hole of her father's stomach. Her childhood was lost, her voice silenced. She was unable to feel the warmth of the sun on her face, or watch puffy white clouds float above the trees, or dance among the other gods during festivals.

With her sixth pregnancy, Rhea decided to trick her husband. Rather than present Kronos with an infant, she handed him a large stone wrapped in blankets. Kronos grabbed the stone without looking and swallowed it. As a result, Rhea gave birth to her sixth child, named Zeus, and hid him far from her husband.

Zeus grew to be a man and avenged his siblings' misery. One night, he secretly put poison in his father's wine, making Kronos vomit out the other trapped offspring. But by then, they were no longer children. They had become full-grown adults.

Demeter worried that one day Persephone, too, would be consumed by tragedy. Although Rhea was a courageous woman to defy her husband, Demeter was convinced she could do a better job at being a mother. Yet, despite trying everything to protect her daughter, De-

meter's greatest fears came to pass. Once Persephone was abducted by Hades to be his bride, it seemed like she was doomed to suffer in the fiery Underworld, never to return.

Betrayal

The winding road over the mountains from Asheville to Tennessee was heavy with low, grey clouds. Henri, Olivia, and I drove for almost five hours, chatting about anything but the fact that we were going to a drug rehab facility. As we descended into the valley, I sensed a loneliness, something I'd often felt in the Appalachians—no matter how many houses or farms we passed, no one seemed to be home. Skirting Nashville on the highway, we came to a small local road that took us through the dreary countryside until we turned down a nameless lane and arrived at our destination.

The admissions building sat in a flat field across from a barn. Henri, Olivia, and I walked like robots into the lobby. We zeroed in on a stiff leather couch and sat down, arranging ourselves in a row. I stood up and moved to a nearby chair so I could be more watchful without twisting my neck. Listening to myself exhale through my nose reminded me of the horses we saw stomping around the front of the barn, their impatient snorts creating white fog in the cold sunlight. I tried to catch Olivia's eye and smile at her. She had that stern, let's-get-this-over-with look on her face. I was ready to throw up.

Every young female staff member who passed through the lobby wore cowboy boots, but I was sure few of them rode any of the horses. They looked more like camp counselors than mental health professionals.

"Huh. Maybe you should have brought your cowboy boots. I can mail them to you," I said.

"It's fine, Mom." Olivia's knee was now bouncing up and down, and she was chewing her lip.

No, it's not! I wanted to scream. I wanted to apologize to Olivia for bringing her to Nashville, this faux country-western city without a cow in sight, where everyone insisted on wearing cowboy boots. I wanted to walk up to the intake worker, tell her this was all a mistake, race with Olivia to the getaway car, and speed all the way home. Instead, the three of us picked through horse magazines, trading them back and forth without reading a word. No other magazines were allowed in the lobby due to ads about drinking or articles about getting skinny and looking sexy—messages too dangerous for addicted minds already obsessed with food or drugs or alcohol or sex.

An older woman with almost waist-length hair came to the waiting room and motioned for us to follow her. We crammed into her tiny office and listened as she explained the rules of the place while she chain-smoked. *How many other staff members here are addicted to cigarettes?* I wondered. After signing page after page of agreements, I was relieved when the therapist arrived, a woman in her mid-thirties who looked professional in her crisp shirt, slacks, and low heels. She asked if she could talk with me. Leaving Henri and Olivia to finish the paperwork, the therapist and I stepped into the hallway, out of Olivia's earshot.

"I wanted to let you know that one month of treatment usually is not enough. I know that's what you have been talking about with Olivia, but if all goes well, she'll need to stay longer."

"Wouldn't she be getting better if 'all goes well'? And, if all goes well, and she is getting better, then she will come home. Right? Isn't that the point? We thought she would be here for a month then return to college mid-January." I looked around for her boss. *Where is the expert with the Ph.D., the one who'll be taking over my job?*

The therapist shrugged her shoulders as if that were an answer. I could feel my body shaking. *What kind of a racket is this? This counselor is too young to have much experience. Plus, she's never taken a daughter to rehab.*

"College is the worst place for Olivia right now, and home isn't much better," she said. I tried to calm down by concentrating on the therapist's gold hoop earrings as she talked. "Olivia needs to stay someplace where she is safe for at least three or four months even to begin recovery."

"And then what?"

"That will be up to her. It takes an average of two years for the brain to heal when drugs have damaged neural pathways. After that, she may decide to stay on here or go to another treatment center in Arizona or Florida."

"But she knows nothing about those places. How can she make that decision? Is she supposed to just point to a place on a map? This is unbelievable!"

"She has her work to do and, frankly, so do you." The therapist's chin was firm, a little too high in the air for my liking.

What "work" was I supposed to do? I'd read multiple self-help books on addiction. I went to Al-Anon meetings and arranged with Henri to begin couples' therapy. We took away Olivia's car and allowance, convinced her to go once a week for drug testing, and got her into rehab. I'd been doing my best to help my daughter turn her life around, hadn't I? My brain began to buzz. This woman sounded like Dr. Holman. *Maybe I should add her to Malvado's long list of "Ann's critics,"* I thought.

Before I could say anything, the therapist spoke again: "Olivia will not be able to contact you for two weeks, but you can call us if you have any questions." I just stared at her and thought, *That's it? We're done here?*

I saw Henri and Olivia walk out of the office, papers signed. It was time to go. We hugged our daughter goodbye in the hallway. Her shoulder muscles were tight, her hug longer than I expected. Tearing up, she tried to hide her trembling lip by biting it. Then donning her let's-get-this-over-with shrug, she turned and threw her backpack over her shoulder. As I watched her walk away, I felt sick. *She thinks she'll be coming home in a month. She has no idea we've betrayed her.*

Before we left the building, Henri went back to the office to ask the intake worker about the slim chance that our insurance might cover any of Olivia's treatment. The therapist and I waited in the hallway.

"Oh, one more thing," she said. "Patients can have a one-hour visit during Christmas. Then you can see Olivia again during the family session the first weekend in January."

"Wait. When we spoke on the phone, you said the meeting would be at the end of December. Henri worked hard to arrange time off from work that week. If the family session is not until the following weekend, he can't get here until early Saturday."

"I'm sorry, but unless he's here Friday night, he won't be able to come at all."

"Just because he misses the two-hour introduction evening, he can't come for the weekend? I thought this place was about helping the families, too."

"I am sorry, but those are the rules."

"But you were the ones who changed the date! This doesn't seem fair. I think I need to speak to the director of the program."

"I don't think that is possible."

"What do you mean it's not possible?" *You little twit! You have no idea who you're dealing with.*

"I can give him a message."

"Alright," I said slowly, deliberately, holding myself back from punching her in the face. "Here is the message: please ask him to call me."

"I don't think that will be possible."

I felt like I was going crazy, and I'd only been at the rehab center a few hours. My daughter was now locked inside. *We agreed to pay an enormous amount for her treatment, and now you're telling me the director can't return a phone call?*

Was I being tested as a parent? Was this part of the "work" I was supposed to be doing, or should I pay more attention to the knot in my stomach? I wanted reassurance. I needed to know I'd made the right decision to bring Olivia to this place. Instead, I felt dismissed, useless— or worse, part of the problem. I turned away from the therapist, walked down the front stairs ahead of Henri, and fumed across the parking lot, stomping on the crunchy, frozen grass.

"I'll drive!" I shouted over my shoulder. My words, low and booming, came from deep inside my chest, rattling the trees like thunder. Henri knew to say nothing. Instead, he handed me the keys. As I sped down the driveway, I lowered the driver's side window and screamed, "Fuck YOU!" toward the building where I imagined the young therapist was already back in her office, smugly reading her email.

Truly Gone

The first time they allowed Olivia to call home, she said she was relieved to be at rehab. I was happy to know she was safe and getting help but looked forward to her return.

After her third week there, she called again. "I've decided to stay at rehab another month. This is where I need to be."

"You mean you won't be going back to college?" I asked.

"Not this semester. It's just really important for me not to come home now. Plus, I'm getting a lot out of being here."

I felt punched in the stomach. Maybe Dr. Holman and the rehab therapist knew what they were talking about. The severity of Olivia's addiction was something I could no longer deny. Part of me knew this was good for her, but another part of me felt like Demeter, refusing to believe her daughter was truly gone.

My family seemed to be imploding. My mother, who was ninety-six, could barely see or hear, and her dementia was getting worse. She would be with us for the holiday, but not really there. Austin wasn't coming home until Christmas Eve, and Olivia wouldn't be home at all. Even making Christmas cookies felt sad to me. It was the first year I'd be making them alone. Unlike Henri, who carefully worked batch after batch of his traditional anise drop cookies until they were perfect, I'd always made a lovely mess rolling out and cutting simple sugar cookies with the kids. We'd bake stars and trees and angels. Olivia and Austin had fun smearing their masterpieces with gobs of icing and colorful sprinkles, saving the best ones to eat with our Christmas Eve dinner.

I grabbed an apron and turned on the *Messiah,* a musical masterpiece conveying the story of the soul's passion and eventual triumph over death. Then, listening to the emotional tides of Handel's oratorio, I became mesmerized as I watched my fingers spread flour back and forth on the kitchen counter.

My mother's rolling pin felt especially heavy in my hands, the dough a little too hard to spread. Everything seemed to be slowing down until I finally stopped and held up one of the metal cookie forms. It was an angel with a circle for a head and a triangle for the dress. To me, it looked just like the drawings of Graffiti Girl I'd seen in Seville. The *Messiah* choir sang, "Come to me!" and I longed to reunite with my daughter. Carefully, I placed the form back into the box. Olivia was my angel—there could be no substitute for her that year.

I burned the Christmas cookies. I wasn't paying attention. Chipping away at the crusty figures still clinging to the cookie sheet, I scraped the remains into the sink and ran the disposal too long. I watched the water from the faucet run down the drain, felt the violent vibration of everything getting pulverized into nothing, wishing I could wash away the guilt I felt for sending my daughter away.

On Christmas morning, Henri, Austin, and I went through the motions of opening presents, but our unspoken sadness made the boxes feel heavy and empty at the same time. The following day, the three of us got up early for the long trip to Nashville. We brought Olivia's Christmas stocking along with a tin of cookies. On the drive, I played the tape Dr. Holman gave Olivia. It explained how drug addiction rewires the brain's neurotransmitters, disrupting normal responses to stress and negatively impacting decision-making processes. I wanted Austin to have a better understanding of Olivia's experience rather than simply think his sister made poor choices.

"Thanks for letting me listen to that," Austin said. "We just finished a section on addiction in my psychology course at college. I hadn't realized how many of my friends have serious problems with alcohol. A lot of people take Adderall to study, too. But Olivia's addiction seems different. How will she deal with this?"

"She's a strong person," Henri said, "but she'll need all of us supporting her to get better."

After we parked, a staff person led us to a cold, empty meeting room with a few round tables and chairs scattered under fluorescent lights. She said it was a requirement that she supervise our tiny family gathering.

"Best to keep your coats on," she said. "We won't be here long enough to turn on the heat. Oh, and the cookies are not allowed. Sorry."

Olivia arrived, and we hugged her tight. She smiled and thanked us as she opened her stocking presents, but the silence in the frigid air surrounding us felt too strange to allow for any real happiness. Before even an hour passed, Christmas with our daughter was over. We said goodbye then left to drive the five hours home. A dull afternoon enveloped our car as we climbed back up and over the mountains.

Austin sat quietly in the back seat for a long time before he spoke. "I feel like I haven't had a sister for years," he said, his voice small and sad. "I lost touch with her and feel bad now. I knew she liked to party. So, when I heard she'd done heroin, I thought maybe she'd tried it once or twice. I didn't know this was happening to her," he said.

"This" was something none of us understood.

Like Persephone, Olivia had been home, then one day, she simply vanished. She wouldn't be returning—not to us, her friends, or college. I realized it would be up to me to dismantle and pack up her room in the off-campus apartment.

A few years earlier, I had to pack up my mother's house when she needed to move. She tried to do it herself, but one day, while carrying a load of towels down the stairs, she tripped, put her head through the sheetrock wall, and landed in the hospital for two weeks. Her house was in shambles. There were dishes and papers all over the kitchen, clothes in piles on her bedroom floor, silverware on the dining table waiting to be polished.

Before she recovered from her injuries, I'd packed all her belongings, delivered the boxes to her new apartment at the retirement home, and put everything away. My mother hated having to rely on me. Later, she complained whenever she couldn't find something, like her travel clock or a spatula, accusing me of giving her things away. Now, I had to clean up for my daughter, but Olivia wasn't around to say thank you—or even complain.

When I arrived at Olivia's apartment, her roommate was gone. I unlocked the door and tiptoed up the stairs, dreading what I would find. There were clothes on the floor (both hers and her boyfriend's), empty marijuana pipes in ashtrays, stacks of barely opened textbooks, a bed crumpled and unmade. Carefully, I unhinged, untangled, and unpinned the posters, photos, scarves, and banners that covered her bedroom walls. When I stripped Olivia's bed, I found Ellie wedged between the bed and the wall. "Ellie the Elephant" was what Olivia called a stuffed animal she had since childhood, the one she curled up with when she was sick, heartbroken, or alone. She had no problem taking Ellie to college but decided against taking her to Nashville as if there would be no room for childishness at rehab. I threw all of Olivia's worldly possessions in giant black bags and boxes, loaded everything into my car, and went home.

The activity of neatly placing her books and photos on shelves in her room at our house was deeply satisfying. It made me feel like I was restoring order to Olivia's chaotic life. I spent hours that day washing load after load of her laundry. When I opened the last bag full of clothes to be done, the stuffed elephant was on top of the pile. Ellie wasn't that dirty, but she had been a witness to the circumstances that had nearly taken my daughter's life. Living between the stained bed sheets, Ellie still smelled of cigarettes. I put her in with the laundry. Maybe I was exercising the last bit of maternal control still available to me. Maybe I wanted to wash away the suffering my daughter had to endure. Maybe I just missed Olivia so much I wanted to hug Ellie without smelling cigarettes.

Asking for Help

I wrote an urgent and professional-sounding email to the director at the rehab facility, insisting he let us arrive early Saturday for the January family session. He acquiesced. For this trip, Henri and I decided to bring a cooler with wine, ice, cheese, and crackers to leave at our hotel—in case the family sessions were too intense.

At the Saturday morning meeting, we gathered with about fifteen other people who all had loved ones in rehab. First, a staff person read the rules for family participants, which included a pledge not to consume alcohol or drugs for the entire weekend. Henri and I sat up a little taller in our seats and swapped guilty looks. Then a psychiatrist presented a talk on addiction and took questions from the group. The assemblage of mothers, fathers, husbands, wives, sisters, brothers, and grandparents listened intently to the speaker, waiting for something hopeful to grab onto. Perhaps this time, recovery would sink in, and everyone could go home to piece their lives back together.

We were led to another room to join our "qualifier," meaning the patient we came to support. Olivia entered the room wearing a big smile and waving across the room to some of her new rehab friends as she headed toward us. We claimed three chairs at one end of a long table and waited for instructions. The first group exercise was to create a family tree. Huddled over a large piece of paper, Henri, Olivia, and I began drawing vertical and horizontal lines resembling a tree, adding names to each branch. At first, this seemed fun and lighthearted. Then we were to highlight any relative who had issues with depression, substance abuse, or other addictive behavior. Henri picked up a blue marker and circled his brother, who suffered from manic depression, then his maternal grandmother and aunt, also depressed. Next was his father, who died by suicide. Brilliant, talented, tortured souls.

I felt a tingling in my hands as I drew a slow red circle around my father's name. Olivia looked at me, surprised. The pieces of her family puzzle were coming together. She began to understand that she was not the only one with problems. We'd always talked openly with our children about depression on Henri's side of the family and the learning differences on my side. Still, it hadn't occurred to me that my father was dependent on alcohol.

Over the past month, I'd read about personality behaviors associated with addiction and the effects on family members. The survival tactics seemed too familiar to me. I was amazed at how easily I identified with several characteristics given to children of alcoholics—like having to guess what constituted normal behavior or being overly self-judgmental and responsible. In the 1950s, my family was picture-perfect to the outside world, but I now saw how each of us suffered—especially my mother. She was so ashamed of my father's controlling attitude toward her that she did her best to hide or excuse his narcissism.

In our house, my father was lord of the manor, captain of the ship, CEO of the family. Each evening after work, he'd pour himself a rather large martini and sit in his chair watching TV. Once the glass was half empty, he'd fix another drink, then often another. He was smooth, rattling the ice in his glass with confidence. He could manage his double martinis for lunch in addition to cocktails before and after dinner. The problem was, he was too good at it.

I rarely saw him drunk, but he always seemed to need a drink. From what I'd read, his personality matched that of an alcoholic, including his inability to form intimate, mature relationships. The few conversations I remember having with him primarily involved me listening to him talk. His generosity was often premeditated, the strings invisible but understood. He demanded loyalty and expected thanks, constantly reminding me that I was lucky he provided everything for me. He was also a fighter and took winning very seriously. In business, in his marriage, with his children—no matter what my father did, he always made a point of coming out on top, even if it hurt the ones he loved.

My father was a strong man. I tried to follow his lead, wanting nothing more than to please him. Unfortunately, he didn't know how to relate to his daughter. His primary objective for sending me away to school was to prepare me to be the wife of a successful business executive, not an independent woman. Even though girls my age in the early 1970s were breaking barriers by attending what had once been all-male colleges, this idea upset him. He even threatened to stop contributing to Dartmouth, his alma mater, if the college admitted women. Strong women unnerved him—thanks, I'm sure, to his dominating mother.

I looked at the names on our family tree and glanced sideways at Olivia. She was busy drawing, bent over the paper. A soft strand of hair was waving in front of her face as she carefully selected each colored pencil. She seemed so childlike, so innocent right then. I longed to scoop her up. I didn't want her to draw another line connecting herself to the lineage of insecurity carried from parent to child on both sides of our families. *What can I do to make up for this?* I wondered.

After lunch, our group went to another room with chairs set in a circle. In the middle of the room were two chairs facing each other. The counselor asked us to think about what we wanted to say to each other, what we took ownership for doing that we now regretted, and what we hoped to see going forward. Rehab residents would be invited to speak with their family members while the rest of the group witnessed these conversations.

"This will be an opportunity for you to issue more than a simple apology," a counselor told our group. "Recovery involves a lot more than getting clean. Families need to reestablish trust and work together if real healing is going to happen." The air felt tight. Everyone avoided eye contact but watched the room to see who would go first.

Listening to other families admit their sins was painful but also liberating. Some stories were shocking, others simply sad. A staff member passed around a box of tissues. Then, it was our turn to sit in the chairs and talk. Olivia began.

"I never wanted to hurt you. I'm so sorry," she said. Henri nodded and told her how much he loved her. Then, he asked her forgiveness for his mistakes and said he was sorry she had to suffer so much. By this time, all three of us were crying.

"I don't know how to begin, Olivia," I said, tears dropping into my lap. "There are so many things I wish I'd done differently now. I tried to give you advice about what you wore or ate or how you acted because I didn't want you to feel hurt by other kids. I thought I was helping you, but now I see I only made you doubt yourself."

After talking, we stood up and hugged. I remember thinking how odd and brave it felt to open our hearts to each other, to be so honest. When I was young, that kind of shared responsibility was not possible in my family. As a result, I grew up accepting that I was at fault for all my shortcomings. My mother believed that if her children had a problem, then they hadn't listened to her advice. But, according to my her, once I had children, any difficulties they had were my fault. I couldn't bring myself to discuss Olivia's addiction with my mother. I knew she would say I was to blame.

On the last day of the family session, we met at a small red barn on the property. There was no heat inside, and the place smelled of sawdust. On one end of a huge room were bleachers. The rest of the space was filled with ropes crisscrossed waist-high from one side to the other in a giant maze. Counselors led everyone into the middle of the room, making sure each person was holding onto some portion of the rope. Then we were blindfolded.

"Good morning," the lead counselor said. "Today, each of you has been blindfolded and placed somewhere along the rope system, which represents addiction. You are to travel along, looking for an exit, but you must always hold the rope. If you have a question, you can raise your hand and whisper it to a staff person. We will let you know when you have ten minutes left to finish. If you don't find the exit in time, the room will explode, and you will die." Everyone chuckled. "Of course, not really," he said, "but addiction is a deadly habit, so you better know how to find a way out. That's what this exercise is about. Begin!"

There were around twenty-five of us all groping for the exit. Even though there was music playing, I could hear feet shuffling. The stiff rope slightly bounced up and down as hands moved along it. At first, people kept running into each other, giggling and apologizing. Occasionally, someone bumped into a wall. I remembered seeing an open barn door to my left just before we were blindfolded. Trying to make my way toward the door, I came face to face with people going the opposite direction, their scents mingling with the cold air. Holding onto the rope, we blindly felt around each other, then kept moving forward. After a while, the counselor announced over a loudspeaker, "Jason found the exit!" Jason was then allowed to take off his blindfold and sit on the bleachers to watch.

One by one, the counselor called out names. People stopped laughing and started getting serious about the game. Then I heard, "Henri found the exit!"

Damn, I thought. *How did he do that?* I felt I'd gone around the room three or four times. At one point, I even raised my hand and whispered to a staff member, "Oh, I get it, there IS no exit," so proud of myself.

"No, you are wrong," she whispered back. "There's an exit. Keep going."

My heart was beating harder, my breath shallow. I wanted to cry. *Why can't I do this?* Then I heard, "Olivia found the exit!" I cheated and pulled my blindfold up just a bit to look around the room. What I saw horrified me. Most people in the group were already seated on the bleachers. Some were even looking bored, waiting for the last losers to "find the exit." Only three people were still in the maze: me, a tall guy with a huge belly, and someone's grandmother.

"You have two minutes before the bomb goes off, and you die," the counselor said over the loudspeaker. "Find the exit!" In desperation and shame, I raised my hand. The lead counselor came to my side, bending his head low to listen.

"I need help!" I whispered.

"That's it! That's the exit," he said. "Congratulations. You can sit on the bleachers now." He patted me on the back and announced over the loudspeaker: "Ann found the exit, just in time! The exercise is now over."

Olivia and Henri rushed to greet me in the middle of the room, and I cried. They embraced me in a tight hug until I could regain my composure and hold up my head. As we walked to the bleachers, I finally heard the music playing throughout the entire game, the Beatles song, "Help!"

DEMETER (RE-IMAGINED)
Mother Rage

In her anger, Demeter shunned the company of gods on Mount Olympus to wander among the mortals. She tore off her headband and threw a dark cloak over her shoulders so no one would recognize her. Exhausted and downhearted, she even began to question her own identity. With a veil over her head, Demeter looked like an old woman.

Soon, four maidens from the palace of Keleos, ruler of Eleusis, came to the well where Demeter was sitting under an olive tree. Not recognizing the goddess, they asked who she was and why she had come to be there. Demeter spun a tale about having been abducted by pirates long ago, but now she hoped to find work taking care of children.

"Our mother has a treasured son," the maidens told her. "If you nourish him until he is grown, you will be rewarded." Demeter took charge of the boy, healing him from a pestilence. To thank the family for their kindness, she planned to secretly place him in the fire to burn away his humanness—a gift of immortality that would make him like the gods. Fire in ancient Greek mythology often symbolized pain and the experience of the Underworld, but it was also associated with energy, assertiveness, inspiration, and purification. One night, Metaneira, the boy's mother, caught Demeter lowering her child into the flames and screamed, which made Demeter yank the child out before completing the transformation.

"Ignorant humans!" Demeter yelled. "You are unable to recognize the difference between future good fortune and bad. Now there is no way for him to avoid death." The goddess rose to her full height, revealing her true self, filling the room with her radiance.

Demeter asked to be honored in Eleusis, but even after Keleois built a splendid temple on top of a prominent hill, she took no joy in it. Instead, Demeter sat on a large stone at the temple entrance looking out over the valley and wept for Persephone. She determined that if she could not save Persephone, she would save no one else. From that point on, Demeter refused to perform her agricultural duties.

Unlike any god or goddess before her, Demeter dared to defy the mighty Zeus. As the fields lay fallow month after month, and the people began to starve, Zeus became alarmed. Unable to persuade Demeter to give up her demands, he agreed to talk to Hades.

Part Three

Confusion as Distraction

Soon after I returned home from Nashville, I attended an Al-Anon meeting and asked a woman named Mary to be my sponsor. She was about my age with curly grey hair and clear-framed glasses that made her eyes look large and wise. A seasoned Al-Anon parent, her comments during our group discussions were compassionate. Plus, her laugh was explosive. Even though I felt vulnerable and unsure of myself, I sensed I could trust her.

While I was attending Al-Anon meetings, I managed to read through the *AA Big Book*, which explains everything about the 12 Steps. The experience at the family weekend, however, made me realize how important it was to actually do the steps, not just read about them. Mary agreed to be my guide through this process. Unlike a therapist, she would be available whenever I needed to talk.

"All you need to do is pick up the phone. If it's inconvenient for me to talk, I'll let you know and call you back later."

"I don't want to burden you," I said.

"You won't be bothering me. This is how it works," Mary said. "I've been where you are. I understand what you're going through, and it can be rough. The point of being a sponsor is partly to help others and partly to help ourselves. I'll be learning along with you, only on a different level. It's the last of the 12 Steps, to be of service and help others."

I'd never heard of such an arrangement. That a stranger would offer to help any time, day or night, and not get paid seemed unbelievable, but this is how AA and Al-Anon survived all these decades. I suddenly felt part of a community and not so alone.

Mary and I met weekly at a coffee shop, tackling the Steps one at a time. I became her student—ready to start over, to surrender. Perhaps I could learn how to be a different kind of mother, or at least understand how to mother a daughter with addiction issues.

"I don't get it," I said to Mary one day after struggling through some of the steps. "For years, I lived in terror every time I picked up the phone and heard Olivia's voice, thinking something was wrong. Now, she calls to say she's happy, then a week later, she says she hates rehab and wants to leave. I'm completely thrown each time."

Mary nodded her head. "You're still trying to anticipate what's going on with her. You can't get ahead of it. You can only deal with things as they come up."

"So, what do I do?" I was leaning onto the table and could feel the back legs of my chair lift off the floor. The whole room felt tilted.

"You don't DO anything." Mary slowly put down her coffee mug. I watched her take off her bulky sweater and place it on top of her tote bag on the floor. When she turned back around, I stared into her eyes, waiting for a better response.

"I'm too upset not to do something," I said.

"And that's just how an addict feels. They can't tolerate the pain and don't have the tools to deal with it, so they look for distractions. We all look for an easy way out."

"This is so confusing. My daughter is fighting for her life, and I'm supposed to stand by and watch?" I could feel my pulse rising and consciously tried to breathe through my nose to calm down.

"Confusion is another distraction. It's pretty simple. The battle isn't with the rehab facility or even with Olivia's addictive behavior. The battle is with yourself," she said.

"What do you mean?"

"You learn to sit with the pain of not being in control—and with your grief. You let it be there, but you don't react to it." Mary then looked at her watch and announced she had to go. "Keep working on the steps," she said. "We'll talk more about this next time."

I didn't understand a thing she was saying, but somehow, I knew she was right. I went home and tried to stay calm. For the next several weeks, storms of anxiety came upon me. First, there'd be a sense of something crackling in the air, and electric currents racing up and down my arms. I'd close my eyes as dark clouds gathered within my head, thunder pounding in my heart. I saw myself like a boat crashing around in an angry black sea, the wind whipping cold waves up and over the bow.

Once the panic attack faded, things got worse. I'd sink lower and lower and stay submerged below the surface of my depression, sometimes for hours. After each of these episodes, I'd try to understand what was happening to Olivia—and to me, but I couldn't hear myself think. Instead, I heard Malvado hissing in my head, "You should have done something. Addiction isn't supposed to happen to 'good' kids from 'nice' families." I couldn't fathom how I would ever feel better, but I believed Mary knew something I didn't. She was living proof that I would survive.

Into the Fire

It was a frigid afternoon, but our living room fireplace made everything feel warm and peaceful. Life was beginning to return to normal. Now in her second month at rehab, Olivia was progressing well through her program. And, for the first time in years, I was sleeping through the night. I looked forward to spending a quiet dinner with Henri after he came home from work. When the phone rang, I thought it might be him.

"Hello, Mrs. Batchelder? This is the nurse at rehab. I'm calling about Olivia." My body braced. "Everything's okay," she said. *They begin every call the same way,* I thought. *But everything is not okay, or they wouldn't be calling so late.*

"There was an accident," the nurse said. "Olivia got too close to a bonfire and caught her jeans on fire. She has second and third-degree burns on the back of her calf. An ambulance took her to the Vanderbilt Burn Unit. Your daughter was very brave. She told the paramedics she was an addict and didn't want morphine or other pain meds. She's resting here in the infirmary. We just wanted to let you know. Hold on a moment, and I'll let you speak with her."

I waited, pressing the phone hard on my ear. *Why is this nurse so cheerful? Am I to be relieved that Olivia was brave?*

"Hi, Mommy." The minute I heard her voice, I forced air into my lungs. I wanted to sound calm.

"Oh, Olivia! What happened?"

"Yeah, well, I had my back to the bonfire, and the fur on my boots caught fire, then my jeans." She was talking fast like she often did when there was a crisis. "I did all the things you told me to do. I dropped and rolled, but the ground was just hard dirt, so that didn't help. I had to wait for a friend to run and get a water bottle to put the fire out. It hurt so bad!"

"Do you want me to come to Nashville now?"

"No, I'm fine… maybe later. The nurse wants me to stay in the infirmary, and I'm pretty tired."

"I'll come tomorrow then."

"That would be better."

I hung up. My heart was still pounding, and I couldn't breathe. I remembered those cheap, short boots—the ones that were so comfy, the ones I bought for her to stay warm in Tennessee. I saw her standing near the bonfire, watched the hungry yellow flames grab her by the ankles. I heard her scream, "I'm on fire!"

Sitting down at my computer, I searched for definitions of a third-degree burn. If I couldn't be in control of what was happening, at least I wouldn't be ignorant about the suffering she faced. Up popped a four-color diagram. In my mind, I pictured the fire catching onto her jeans, then burning through "the first layer of skin (the epidermis), then the layer underneath (the dermis), finally scorching the subcutaneous tissue—the exposed nerves, the blood vessels, muscle, fat and sweat glands beneath." I realized her scars would be permanent, just like all the emotional scars she already carried. I felt nauseous and closed the computer.

"She could have died!" Henri said when I called to tell him.

"I know," I said, feeling anxious—as if I was supposed to have an answer or was somehow responsible for this tragedy. "I told her I'm going there tomorrow."

Along the highway to Tennessee, I kept imagining Olivia rolling in the dirt, trying to put out the flames, her skin melting away. It made me sad to think how often she struggled in her young life. Suffering from a burn, I realized, is like the experience of depression. Without natural protective layers, skin and psyche are both left raw and exposed, extremely sensitive to things usually taken for granted—like air or blood flow, rejection or loss.

When I arrived at the same conference room where we'd visited Olivia during Christmas, I was surprised to see her hobble in on crutches, being brave. It was still hard for me to believe she was struggling with addiction, that she'd been in rehab since early December, that she wouldn't return to college anytime soon and might not be coming home at all. Now, she had to suffer from a horrible burn. Some people run away from fire, I thought. Olivia wears it.

We were only allowed to visit for an hour that day. Sitting together on a cold leather couch, Olivia rested her injured leg on a chair and swung her other leg onto my lap. I began massaging her calf, imagining we were sitting at home in our living room. I wanted to stay there all day—touching my daughter, reassuring her, hearing about her accident, listening to her gossip about the people she'd met, and describe the food, the beds, the counselors, the therapy sessions, the emptiness, the work, the fear, the hope of rehab. Too soon, I had to leave. Too soon, I had to let go. With her in rehab, so far away and in pain, I no longer understood my role as her mother. This was new territory for me.

Breaking the Chain

After Olivia's accident, I'd lie awake in bed most of the night with my hand on my heart, fighting to keep Malvado from entering my thoughts. Just before dawn, I'd roll over and watch the sky turn paler by the hour until a cheerful sun had the audacity to pop up and over the mountains. While I pretended to sleep, I could hear Henri tiptoe out of the room and leave for work. Sometimes, I'd sleep till noon. Other times, I'd sit cross-legged on an oversized leather chair in the living room and study the motionless horizon, my coffee cup untouched and growing cold.

What saved me from total despair during those gloomy months was seeing Mary. She expected me to show up each week to continue working through the 12 Steps. We'd meet at a cafe where millennials sat by the windows to work on their laptops or settle themselves in lumpy chairs to read in front of a fake fireplace. Community meetings often took place in the corners, and once a week, a group of older ladies met at the same table to play cards. A few times, I'd recognized someone there from my Al-Anon group. Mary and I fit right in.

One day, I listened to Mary's jangling earrings as she approached my table and watched as she sat down. She opened her notebook, gave me a big smile, and asked, "So, what did you write about for this Step?"

I took a long slurp from my latte, then looked up at her. "I don't know if I can honestly do this Step. How do you turn your life over to 'a god of your understanding' if you are not a religious person?" Mary crinkled her face into a knowing grin. Even though we were about the same age, I always felt like such a novice around her.

"This is a hard one," she said. "But it's important. It's about giving up the idea that you are God."

"Well, of course, I know I'm not God." My tone was both amused and annoyed.

"Really?" Now Mary wasn't playing.

"Let's just say I don't think God can handle things for me," I said, more serious this time.

Mary nodded. "How about this. What if you could simply decide to accept life as it is without trying to control the outcome? Can you take that step?"

I told her I could try. I only started going to Al-Anon to support Olivia. I wanted to see what I could learn. My hope was that if Olivia and I were both engaged in working on our own 12-Step programs, she might not feel so alone in her journey. Plus, if we shared a common language, it might be easier for me to encourage her to stay in recovery.

At first, that was true. Olivia and I would laugh on the phone about our experiences going to group meetings, discuss various ways to define "higher power," or agree that we both hated the way people had to label themselves ("Hi, I'm Lucy. I'm an alcoholic"). I was proud of the progress we'd made in our mother–daughter relationship, but the 12-Step process was proving to be more challenging than I'd anticipated. Rather than talk about Olivia, Mary kept bringing the focus back to me, to my recovery. I began reflecting on the exercises Henri, Olivia, and I did during the family weekend at the rehab center back in January, our family tree of addiction, depression, grief, and struggle. The deeper I probed, the more I began to see something else Olivia and I shared: generations of women in our family who had similar fears.

My mother bucked convention when she was a young woman. She could have had the perfect wedding in 1941. All the arrangements were in place for it to happen at her parents' home in Seattle during Christmastime. Four months before the big event, she took a train to San Francisco where my father's battleship was stationed. One night, she and my father drove to Nevada with an address in hand. Arriving at their destination in the wee hours, they woke up a justice of the peace and were married in the man's kitchen. The judge's wife, bleary-eyed and none too pleased, made coffee.

My mother's mother did something similar. Even though she grew up during the turn of the twentieth century, she had a mind of her own. She met my grandfather while visiting her sister in Seattle. When her father caught wind of this courting, he wired money for her to take the train home to Houston right away. Instead, she used the money to buy a new plume for her hat and eloped.

Women in my family were feisty when they were young, but they became uncharacteristically fearful once they had children. My mother constantly fed me terrifying bits of information to ensure I'd stay guarded against danger. When I'd least expected it—like driving together to the mall or setting the dinner table—she'd ambush me with some bizarre fact that would splat on the wall of my brain like a paintball, the stain remaining there forever.

Pretty soon, I couldn't go outside without watching for snakes known to "paralyze their prey on the first strike" or walk in the rain-soaked grass during a storm without thinking that "lightning can travel hundreds of yards across a field, killing everything in its path." My mother was not a fearful person, but she made sure I understood that disaster was only a step away, and that I needed her and her anxious advice to survive in this dangerous world. Her mother had been the same way. She never let my mother learn how to ride a bicycle—too risky. It was as if the same need for maternal concern and vigilance had been handed down through the ages.

While I was away at boarding school, I felt free from my mother's anxieties. Having children, on the other hand, was a leap of faith for me. I prayed for a soft landing. Growing up, I never had babysitting jobs and was clueless about infants. I secretly worried I would drop my child one day while changing diapers. When I was pregnant with Austin and told to stay on bedrest for six months, I became extremely cautious. I planned every trip to the bathroom, walking slowly and deliberately to avoid accidentally dislodging the life growing inside me. Even though I kept working as an editor, I changed my identity, my reason for being. I was now a vessel to grow a child.

From that point on, even though I did everything I could to maintain my children's well-being, I worried I would let them down. I donned the heavy cloak of fear, the same one passed down to me from my mother and her mother. I didn't trust my children to have their own problems and solutions, their own destinies. I assumed it was up to me to keep them from the dark waters of life. Olivia was the product of this female line of spirited women who were also cursed with messages of guilt and failure. One day, I realized, if she had children, she would inherit this definition of motherhood. I knew it was time to break that chain—for her sake and for her daughter's daughters. I had no idea how to do this, but just before my mother died, she showed me the way.

Letting My Mother Go
—And Stay

I adored my mother, and we were close when I was growing up, but she became bitter after my father died. She was eighty-three and lived with my father for sixty years. Throughout their marriage, she endured his verbal abuses and infidelities, but the final blow was when he left her all alone in the world. Then, the hurt and humiliation she'd harbored all those years spilled out toward me. I became a failure in her eyes, both as a daughter and a mother. I'd hoped that with my father's death, we would be able to have more mother–daughter fun together. Instead, over the thirteen years that followed, we became increasingly disconnected. I couldn't do anything right.

She was "sickened," for example, that I let Austin grow his hair into a big, bushy tangle of curls one year during middle school. Not wanting to be embarrassed by him in front of her friends, my mother refused to let him visit her at the retirement home. Had she learned her granddaughter, whom she adored, had been addicted to heroin, I am sure she would have insisted I put Olivia under house arrest for the next ten years. Instead, I told my mother Olivia was going to a treatment center to help with her depression.

Mom was ninety-six years old and living in a retirement home in Asheville when Olivia was about to go to rehab. Before departing, she went to visit her grandmother for lunch. Not half an hour afterward, my mother called me, outraged.

"I just want to ask you a question. Is that a tattoo I saw on Olivia's wrist?"

"Yes, Mother… it is."

"Well, I am disgusted! How could you let your daughter do such a thing? I am telling you right now, you have got to get control of her, or she'll be sorry."

"Sorry" seemed like such a simple word to me at that moment. My mother had no idea of the trouble Olivia was already in, the life-and-death struggle of her addiction. Mom was worried about a small tattoo on Olivia's wrist while Hades already had his hand tightly wrapped around my daughter's ankle. Mom didn't see me, and she didn't see her grandchildren. All she saw was a reflection of herself—an image she worked hard all her life to keep spotless.

I held the phone away from my ear as my mother continued to rant. Then she hung up on me. She'd never done that before. I placed my cell phone on the dining table, walked to the window, and stood for a long time watching one lonely cloud after another drift from west to east above the mountains. My eye caught the shadow of a massive hawk slowly floating over the field below our house. I knew there would be no songbirds at the feeder for the next few days.

Shortly after Olivia's accident with the bonfire, my mother started experiencing a series of mini strokes. Often, she became disoriented. Other times, she was lucid. For two weeks, I spent almost every waking moment with her. I couldn't stop touching her, trying to register every detail—the way she smelled of Pond's cold cream, how beautiful her face looked as she napped in the afternoon light, the way her powder-blue eyes sparkled when she told a joke, her thick white hair still wavy and glamorous despite not being able to get her weekly perm at the retirement-home beauty shop. During that time, something changed between us. We often hugged and patted each other's backs. There was a softness, an openness between us. It was as if we finally forgave each other for being human.

One morning, before going to visit my mother, I got a call from Olivia's surgeon at Vanderbilt Hospital. Her wound was not healing correctly, the doctor told me. She would need a skin graft within the next few days since the surgeon was leaving town for a conference at the end of the week. From what I'd heard, having a skin graft was excruciatingly painful. *My daughter will literally be skinned alive.* I tried not to think about it. I didn't ask Olivia if she wanted me to come. I packed my bag.

"You know your mother is going to die," Henri said that evening, a mix of medical fact and deep sorrow in his voice.

"She's ninety-six. I don't expect her to live forever."

"I mean, it's only a matter of time before she has a major stroke. It could happen tomorrow or weeks from now," he said. "I'll be here, and so will the hospice nurse, but you need to understand this."

The following day when I rode the elevator up to my mother's apartment, I noticed my hands clenched inside my coat pockets. I didn't want to leave. I explained to her that Olivia needed an operation, and she would be in the hospital for several days.

"You must go to her," my mother said. "I'll be fine." We stood and hugged each other. I noticed that her body no longer towered over me. Now, her bent frame only reached as high as my shoulders.

"Don't go anywhere until I get back," I said and winked at her. She smiled back. Neither of us could bring ourselves to talk about the end of her life.

"Now, listen," my mother said, a phrase that always caught my attention growing up. It meant she was either about to say something serious or important—or that I had done something wrong. She took my hand and looked me in the eye for a long time. I had no idea what to expect. Then, slowly, quietly, she said, "You're going to get through this."

I didn't realize how many years I'd waited to hear her say that instead of telling me all the things I'd done wrong. For the first time, she expressed sincere faith that I could handle whatever might happen in my life—her death, Olivia's illness, all of it. I repeated the phrase as I walked down the stairs, out to the parking lot, and into the day without her. It was the greatest gift she'd ever given me.

I pointed the car toward Nashville and drove. Thankfully, Route 40 is a straight shot running directly from Asheville over the Blue Ridge Mountains and down into the Tennessee Valley, so I didn't have to pay attention to directions. My car accelerated when I thought of Olivia, wanting to race to Vanderbilt Hospital to be with her, then decelerated as I thought of leaving my mother forever. With each mile, I felt torn in two, my heart oscillating, my tears blurring the highway. I followed the red taillights in front of me until the sky turned from deep blue to black.

Burn Unit

When I arrived at the hospital, Olivia and a counselor from rehab were standing outside the entrance waiting for me. I ignored Olivia's scowl and gave her a hug.

She whispered to me, "You didn't need to come." For once, I decided not to take her comments personally. After checking in, we said goodbye to the counselor and sat with several other families in a vast waiting room. The vaulted ceiling magnified the chatter, ringing telephones, and booming announcements made over a loudspeaker. After a while, a nurse called Olivia's name, and we both jumped up.

"You can stay here," the nurse said to me. "We'll let you know when you can go to the recovery room to see your daughter." She motioned for Olivia to follow her, and I stood in the middle of the waiting room, watching them march through a broad set of swinging doors, turn a corner, then disappear.

To the right was another door with a little sign that said "Chapel." I entered the small, dimly lit room and shut the door. It was quiet as a coffin. Stripped bare of denominational adornments, there were a few rows of wooden pews and a simple table at the front of the room. You could drag whatever religious baggage you wanted into this space. It felt inclusive, open for interpretation. On the very back row, I sat on a cushion—it was a deep, royal purple, the kind of color you might find in a Hindu or Buddhist temple. Folding my legs under me, I sat tall and began the slow, meditative breathing I often practiced in yoga classes, hoping to calm myself. I figured it wouldn't hurt to ask for Olivia's safety during her operation. After registering my prayer, I wondered if there was anyone to hear it.

I'd always been a seeker, sometimes even a believer. I loved going into tiny, empty chapels or soaring cathedrals in Europe whenever I traveled. To find a quiet sanctuary after tromping around a busy, dirty city like Paris or Barcelona was like stepping into my soul. The light felt personal. Even the air seemed mysteriously holy. In America, most Protestant churches felt deadened and lonely to me, forgotten places from Monday through Saturday, with everyone too busy to stop in for a chat with God. Perhaps that's why no one interrupted me as I sat for over an hour in the Vanderbilt Hospital chapel. It was Tuesday, not Sunday.

In the chapel, I drifted in a sleepy, meditative state, until I heard someone announce my name over the loudspeaker. I hurried down the hall, then stood at the recovery room door, just out of sight. A nurse was asking Olivia if she wanted another shot of morphine. Olivia nodded yes then stared at the needle pricking her arm. Like a voyeur, I watched my daughter close her eyes and tilt her head back as she felt the all-too-familiar rush of relief. Unlike getting high on the streets, this time, the drug was sanctioned, necessary.

"Hi, Mom," she said when she finally opened her eyes and saw me. "How are you?"

"It wasn't good. They were supposed to give me a block to do the skin graft, right? Well, it wore off before they could wheel me into the recovery room. I've never been in such pain. I was screaming and crying. It hurt so much, Mom. I'm glad you weren't here to see that."

I just stood there, not knowing what to say. Because Olivia was in addiction recovery, the doctors had assured me she would not receive a needle with pain medicine, the risk of relapse being too great. In the hallway, a nurse stopped me to apologize.

"I'm sorry about the block. We had to use the needle. Olivia couldn't have tolerated the pain caused by the skin graft surgery." But she did tolerate it, I wanted to say—all the way from the operating room to the recovery room. I ached for her, hating that once again she had to be brave, hating that all her life she had to work so hard to feel okay.

People often think anyone with an addiction issue must be weak, but I was coming to see that wasn't true. No one chooses to be addicted. At first, drugs are used in an attempt to relieve excruciating pain and emptiness. And, for a while, that works. But once the body gets used to requiring a daily dose of opioids, it needs stronger and stronger doses to maintain equilibrium, to simply feel normal. Drug use becomes a necessity, not a joy ride.

Unlike mending skin or bones, addiction is difficult to heal—it doesn't simply get better over time. Ample tools and support are needed for recovery. The psychological and sometimes physical pain related to depression and addiction is genuine and can be chronic, and the healing process complicated and lifelong.

For over a year, Olivia had tried to let go of drugs—first moving to Asheville, then forcing herself to go through withdrawal on her own, signing up for rehab, and going through the 12 Steps. She had worked hard every day to face down her cravings, anxiety, and depression. Then, a nurse stuck a needle with opioid medicine into her arm, reminding her how much easier it is to just let drugs take over. Her mind was no match for her body's response.

DEMETER (RE-IMAGINED)
Persephone's Choice?

At the insistence of Zeus, Hades reluctantly agreed to relinquish his bride, providing Persephone did not eat anything in the Underworld. If she did, she would have to stay with Hades forever. Persephone understood this ancient law. But just before she returned to Earth, Hades said he would honor her as his queen if she remained. Then, he gave her three pomegranate seeds. And she ate them.

Did Hades trick her? Did Persephone have a lapse in judgment, or did she choose to stay? Homer's recounting of the myth is unclear. Yet, with that act, Persephone became ruler of her own world, capable of making her own decisions. It was then that Demeter realized she was no longer the mother of a child.

Persephone ate the pomegranate seeds, which would have sealed her fate. But Zeus worried about Demeter. If she did not return to her duties, the mortals would continue to suffer and no longer trust the gods. To appease both Demeter and Hades, Zeus let Persephone live on Earth with her mother but only if she agreed to spend three months in the Underworld each year.

During those three months, Demeter craved her daughter's return. Heartbroken, she let the world become dark and barren. But each spring, when Persephone emerged from the Underworld, Demeter rejoiced and allowed the land to grow rich and fertile again with new life. And, so, the seasons came to be.

The Bargain

After getting a morphine high in the recovery room, Olivia wanted more. She spent the next five days focusing on little else. Rather than swallow the pain pills the nurses gave her each day, Olivia secretly held onto them. The nurses never noticed—she was that good. Once I realized my daughter was relapsing, I told Olivia I had to get something from my car in the parking garage. I needed time away from her so I could think.

The red taillights flashed as I opened the door and slid into the driver's seat. I couldn't bring myself to drive anywhere. I was a stranger in Olivia's world and afraid of getting lost again. After sitting in the dark for a long time, I called my sponsor, Mary.

"Hi. It's Ann. I'm sorry to bother you, but do you have time to talk now?" We'd always arranged to meet at the coffee shop once a week, but this was the first time I'd called her. I felt like an addict—trembling, terrified, wanting to race home, wanting a cigarette or a drink or anything to make me feel better.

"Yes, this is fine, and you're not a bother. What's up?"

"I'm at the hospital, in the parking garage. Before I left Olivia's room, the nurse came in to administer her pain meds—Oxycodone, I think—for her skin graft. She palmed her drugs."

"She what?"

"She made it look like she was swallowing her medication but kept the pill in her hand so she could take several doses together and get high. I watched her."

"Are you sure?"

"Full disclosure? I read her journal while she was out of the room, getting her wound redressed. She wrote that she'd been saving two to three doses at a time to get high. She left her journal opened on the bed right in front of me as if she wanted me to see it."

"A part of her probably did."

"In a way, I don't blame her, but I can't believe the pain she has to endure while waiting hours to get enough meds to get high."

"That's addiction," Mary said. Nothing surprised her. She was a rock.

"I want to confront Olivia, talk to her, but I don't want her to know I read her journal."

"But you did read it. And, anyway, she could deny holding the pills. So, if you want to have an impact, you'll have to see her doing it and confront her when it happens. But even then, what do you hope to accomplish?"

"I don't want her to keep secrets from me."

"But she is. And until she can control her impulses, she'll probably continue to do this. A part of her knows exactly what she's doing, but the neural pathways in her brain are still firmly rooted toward short-term rewards."

"I don't want this for her."

"I know. Still, she will only come clean about it when she's ready—or she won't. You can't force her or watch her every move waiting to catch her in the act whenever she slips up. She's going to slip up. That's part of recovery."

Sliding down into my car seat, I stared at the painted cement wall in front of me. *What do they call that color? Taupe? Is it grey or brown? Why can't I decide?* I looked over at the garage opening and noticed the evening fog created a burnt orange aura around the exit sign. Tears were falling onto my chest.

"I feel so deflated."

"She feels the same way—only ten times more. Keep believing in the person she's trying to be, hold that long-term vision for her. Trust her process."

"So, what do I do?" I hated myself for asking this question again.

"You have to wait," Mary said. "When and if the opportunity presents itself, talk to her about hiding the pills in her hand. Otherwise, focus on breathing through this. That's your job right now. Recovery takes a long time. She may keep running into the fire for a while, rather than run away from it, no matter how many times she gets burned."

When I left the parking garage and returned to the hospital, Malvado was waiting for me in Olivia's room. He was standing in a corner smoking a cigarette, dropping his ashes on the floor. Beads of sweat formed on his bald head while his eyes stayed fixed in a squint. The putrid stench of him hurt my nose. I wasn't surprised my mind resurrected Malvado at this moment. Still, I tried to ignore him.

A nurse stopped by to tell me Olivia was getting her leg wrapped and would be back soon. I sat on the edge of the stiff recliner chair, squeezing my hands together in my lap. I wondered for the hundredth time, *How did she get here?* But I knew. I'd watched Olivia's depression progress through high school, saw how she'd tried to soothe herself with drugs as best she could in college, then witnessed her incredible resolve to become healthy and whole. Her recovery journey was just beginning, so was mine. We both had much to learn.

Olivia entered the room in a wheelchair, her leg encased in a huge bandage from the knee down. Easing herself onto the bed, she propped up her leg with three white pillows, then gave me a weak smile.

"How are you doing?" I asked.

"It hurts. This whole thing sucks, actually."

"You mean your burn?"

"I mean all of it, Mom."

Malvado walked over to the window and leaned against it, waiting to hear what I would say next—what brilliant words of wisdom, what consoling comments, what motherly advice. I heard his thoughts: "See, you are so inept as a mother, you can't even think of something to say." He was right, I had no words. Instead, I took a deep breath and sat in silence next to her on the bed, forcing myself to be present to my daughter's misery rather than try to fix it.

On my last day at the Vanderbilt Burn Unit, I brought food from a local deli so Olivia and I could have a picnic lunch together.

"Someone will pick you up in the morning to take you back to rehab,"

I said. "I have to drive home this afternoon and see Gammy. She's had another stroke, a big one. She might not live long."

Olivia said she couldn't imagine losing a mother, and I felt tears rising from my heart. She reached across the hospital bed to hug me. It was the first time I had allowed my daughter to comfort me. I leaned into her.

We finished lunch, and then a nurse entered with medication. I watched as Olivia expertly pretended to swallow the pill and then casually laid it on the sheet next to her hip so the nurse couldn't see. But I was on that side of the bed and picked it up.

"Oh, look," I said, handing the pill to Olivia. "You must have dropped this." Olivia shot me a knowing glance before she swallowed the pill. The nurse looked surprised but went about her business. Once we were alone in the room, I sat on Olivia's bed. She stared at the ceiling.

"What was that about?" I asked.

"I don't know. I'm sorry. I just wanted to get high, and I figured it would be okay since the doctors gave me the medicine anyway."

"Seriously?"

She promised not to do it again. I sighed. She looked away. Sadness sat between us like a vase of dying flowers. We both knew she would do it again. In the past, I would have reminded her that she had choices, resources, and tools to deal with potential relapses. Instead, I held her hand.

"This is your life now, Olivia. It's going to be up to you to be honest with yourself," I said. "But one thing I do know—you're going to get through this." I put on my coat to leave and gave her a long hug goodbye. I noticed a faint outline against the wall as I walked toward the door. The figure that was once Malvado had faded—he was barely visible.

The Silence of Trust

While I was in Nashville, a major stroke put my mother in bed for the rest of her days. With her face fixed in a lopsided frown and her right limbs useless, she could only utter one word at a time. Once home, I spent the next several days by her side—holding her hand, helping her eat ice cream, applying Vaseline to her cracked lips. Her body was shutting down, the hospice nurse explained. Yet even in that state, she had a sense of humor. Using smiling eyes and a sarcastic word, she still tried to make everyone who visited laugh and feel at ease.

I had returned to Asheville on a Tuesday to see my mother. By Saturday, she was dead. It was overcast on the morning I got a call from the retirement home saying we should come immediately. When Henri and I arrived at the parking lot, I received another call that my mother had just died. We rode the ridiculously slow elevator to her floor and met the hospice nurse in the hallway. A sweet Southern woman, she held my hand and told me she sang "Amazing Grace" as my mother quietly "passed." I was heartbroken that I couldn't have been there, upset that I hadn't been the one to sing to her, but grateful she left this world listening to such a tender song.

In the room, I found my mother serenely present but not present, still lying in her single bed, the same bed that had been mine when I was growing up. Never one to throw anything useful away, Mom insisted on keeping that bed as she and my dad moved from house to house over the years. She looked serene with her white hair floating below the familiar wooden headboard. An old, pink blanket from my childhood covered her bony frame. Her mouth, slack-jawed and open, didn't move. No air filled her lungs or raised her chest, and the color had drained from her cheeks. The taut skin on her face was an ivory color that was still beautiful in the quiet morning light. The vibrant, funny, tough woman I loved was gone, but when I put my hand on her shoulder, her back was still warm where the stagnant blood had pooled inside her body. I crawled onto the single bed, placed my arm over her stiff body, and gently sang to her—as if she was the child now, as if we could both find comfort in that bed.

After losing my mother, I drifted through months of sadness. The confusion I'd felt about our relationship now was heavy with loneliness. I had nowhere to place my affection, hurt, or adoration. I didn't want to talk with anyone. Instead, I spent quiet hours writing in my journal or rereading books by my favorite Buddhist teachers. Settling down to absorb their wisdom again, I'd put my hand on my chest to feel the drumming of my heart. Sometimes, I let myself cry.

It's natural to avoid pain, but according to Buddhist thinking, such avoidance is at the core of suffering. I thought I understood this principle, but I was blind to the many ways I'd run away from pain, especially regarding Olivia. I didn't know how to sit with my discomfort, allow it, or learn from it. Instead, I thought it was my job to protect my daughter—to dampen her burning desires and save her from being consumed by the flames of addiction. I tried my best to patch up her Achilles heel, where depression took hold and dragged her down, sucking energy and light from her being.

Once I accepted that I couldn't prevent her pain, I still tried to control her healing. I figured that if I could research her problems, find people to help her, and learn to be a better mother, then at least Olivia would have a chance. But I was too attached to the outcome, the way I thought things should be.

It wasn't until I read a book by Buddhist teacher Kevin Griffin called *One Breath at a Time: Buddhism and the Twelve Steps* that I began to see a bigger picture. Recovery is not about trying to fix something broken, he explains. Instead, it involves finding ways to tolerate that which, at first, seems intolerable. Addiction is part of the human condition—not something unique to those who abuse drugs or alcohol. And recovery can have as much to do with the Buddhist practice of mindfulness as developing self-awareness through working the 12 Steps. Both approaches "hold up a lamp in the dark."

He describes the Buddhist Four Noble Truths like this: The first truth says there is pain in life, but we can be free from suffering. The second truth acknowledges that all humans have a ceaseless desire for self-gratification, but it is possible to learn restraint. In other words, we can learn to let go of cravings and desires—the causes of suffering. The third truth says that when we finally let go of our attachments, it is possible for pain to dissolve.

The fourth truth is the key to the Noble Truths. It is a blueprint for letting go, a way to end suffering by following the Eightfold Path. To do this, Buddhists spend their lives becoming aware of and then practicing what is called right view, right intention, right livelihood, right action, right speech, right effort, right mindfulness, and right concentration. This, to me, seemed impossible. *How could anyone expect to be that perfect?* I was hungry to learn more. I heard Kevin Griffin was leading a five-day silent retreat at a dharma center outside Asheville. It was primarily for people in recovery, but anyone was welcome to come. I signed up.

Having never been to a silent retreat, I had no idea what to expect. I packed my books, journal, sketchpad, sun hat, and an iPad full of podcasts about mindfulness. After driving for an hour into the mountains outside Asheville, I came to a tranquil place tucked deep in a cove called Southern Dharma. There were six rustic cabins, a meditation room, and a large building containing the dining hall. Also on the property was a tiny garden and a path leading up to a clearing in the woods. I walked across the narrow parking lot and climbed the stairs to the dining hall for our orientation. I was one of the few moms there. Most of the other participants were young and recovering from drug or alcohol addiction.

"Everyone will be assigned a chore each day," Kevin said. "After breakfast, we will meet at 9 a.m. and meditate until noon, and then I will give a dharma talk. We'll have lunch and meditate again until 4. After dinner, there will be another talk and a final meditation until bedtime.

All the meals will be silent. You are not to speak to anyone the entire time, including your roommate. Also, no electronics, reading, journaling, or listening to music." I looked around the room to see if anyone else thought this was a joke. I figured six hours a day of sitting in meditation was simply not possible for me. Before this retreat, I'd only managed to sit twenty minutes at a time. Plus, not speaking for days on end would be like being locked in a closet with myself. My fingers tightened on the car key in my pocket.

The following morning, I sat on a meditation pillow for what seemed like an eternity. All I could think about was the tingling in my feet, hoping I could eventually stand up again despite the lack of blood circulation to my legs. Opening my eyes, I looked around to see if anyone else seemed uncomfortable. *Either they've all done this a million times, or they're good at hiding their agony,* I thought. The more I focused on my legs, the worse they felt. I tried to take deep breaths to quiet my thoughts, but my mind kept screaming for me to move something, anything. This went on for hours. Finally, Kevin spoke. Everyone in the room released a collective sigh, shifted a bit, then settled down to listen to his talk. I couldn't hear what he was saying. All I cared about was getting to lunch. I didn't think I could take another long session that afternoon, followed by a third meditation after dinner. But I did.

After surviving the first day, I decided to try another day, then another. With each meditation, I became less cranky. I found I could watch my thoughts come and go like waves, rising and falling away. If I worried about Olivia, I felt my body become tense. Other times, I smiled, recognizing the sound of a mockingbird or wood thrush outside. I listened to air traveling through my nose and down my throat or noticed if someone near me adjusted their posture. Sometimes, I felt tears slip down my cheeks.

By the fourth morning, I looked forward to the time spent in the meditation room with the other participants. Even though no words passed between us, I felt a sincere affection toward these souls. And I appreciated what Kevin had to say. Learning about Buddhism from the perspective of addiction and the 12 Steps from the perspective of Buddhist philosophy brought new clarity. I began to see how all humans are on the spectrum of addiction and, as is often said at retreats such as this one, "We're all just walking each other home."

On the last day of the retreat, having no morning chores, I chose to hike about a quarter mile up a hill to a large clearing in the woods. On the edge of the field there was a hammock strung up between two trees. I settled into it, half dozing while a late May sun danced on my face. At one point, there seemed to be a presence near me. Turning my head and opening my eyes, I looked into a coyote's face only ten feet away.

I told myself not to move but felt too vulnerable lying down. Slowly, I sat up, keeping my eyes on the coyote the entire time, ready to bolt if he attacked. Instead of being frightened by me, he took two steps forward. He was scrawny, looking as if he'd circled the forest too many times, scavenging for food. His tail was still, his pointed ears up and alert. We locked eyes for what seemed to be forever, waiting for the other to make a move.

Then I did the only thing that felt natural—what I often did as a mother—I started talking. I talked in run-on sentences, a steady stream of motherly verbiage. I told this creature he was totally out of line. I told him, matter-of-factly, that I didn't appreciate him being so close, that I was going to stand up and leave, but I wasn't going to run because I didn't want him to get excited and tell all his coyote friends lurking around in the forest to join him in chasing me. I told him what he was doing was threatening, and I didn't like it. I was clear and firm, getting louder and more insistent, gathering confidence the more I spoke.

I kept on like this until he rolled his eyes and trotted off, but he didn't go far away. While I hurried back down the path to the meditation hall, I could see him in the woods. He was following me—walking parallel but at a distance like Malvado used to. I will never know if he was rabid or sick, a trickster or a messenger. All I knew was that I trusted myself to face my fear that day. I had made a coyote back off—and I could do it again if I needed to.

Points of Change

After rehab, Olivia transitioned to a halfway house for a few weeks, then decided to remain in Nashville. She found an apartment with an AA friend, got a restaurant job, and stayed sober. Working next to her at the deli counter was a college kid. They laughed a lot and enjoyed the same music. During a call home, she told me she was starting to have a crush on him. The weekend before Thanksgiving, they went out. They kissed.

The boy wasn't there on Monday morning when she went to work. She was prepping the salad station, wondering why he was late. Her boss called all the staff into the back room to make an announcement: the boy was dead. Olivia was convinced he was wrong. She ran outside and tried to text him—again and again. She couldn't stop crying at work, so her boss let her go home. She was still sobbing when she called us at noon.

"He might have been drinking. It doesn't matter," Olivia said. "He tripped at the top of the stairs at his parents' home, fell to the bottom, and hit his head hard on the wall. His younger brother tried to save him but couldn't. He died later that night in the hospital with his mother holding his hand. Mom, I was the last person he kissed." Her sobs became a low moan, a sound raw and foreign to me. I imagined her sitting on the floor of her rented apartment in a trance—her face swollen, her eyes red from crying, rocking back and forth inconsolably. I gripped the phone, waiting for her to come up for air. I told her to get in the car and come home early for Thanksgiving.

Olivia cried all the way from Nashville to our house. When she arrived, we hugged her, held her, and let her cry more. The holiday itself was a blur. Austin couldn't make it home, and friends invited us to their house to share Thanksgiving dinner. That evening, Olivia didn't drink any of the wine passed around. She smiled and engaged in conversations but kept getting up from the table to use the bathroom and make phone calls. Each time she stood up, I tried not to move my head as I watched her leave.

Henri and I stayed close to Olivia all weekend. We ate turkey sandwiches, walked in the woods, and watched movies. On Saturday afternoon, we gathered in the living room in front of the fireplace. Henri and I read. Olivia sprawled on the rug with a large drawing pad. She painted a phoenix rising from the ashes to give to the boy's mother at the memorial. No one spoke. Instead, we let the warmth of the fire draw us closer. We felt like a family again. Sad as it was, I didn't want that day to end.

On Sunday, Olivia returned to Nashville and called a few days later, complaining that the AA meetings were boring. This was a tip-off for me that she was heading toward a relapse or was already in one. The pattern was always the same. First, she'd call with a problem, then another. Then she'd call to say she was too busy to talk. Then she'd stop calling for weeks and wouldn't answer her text messages. The worst part of Hell is not the torturous fires, I realized. It's the separation from those who you love. I thought if I could somehow relieve her pain, she would return to me.

The more I tried to reach Olivia, the more I felt myself spiraling down, imagining the worst. *I can't allow this to be happening,* I told myself. To relieve my anguish, I researched for hours online, trying once again to figure out how to fix things. I found articles like "How to Stay Sober" or "Tips on Talking to Your Addicted Child"—anything I could use to help Olivia fight her fight. Still, I knew my efforts would be futile if she refused to pick up the phone.

Over the years, I'd witnessed my own relapses many times. Thinking I'd made progress, priding myself on being able to let Olivia make her own choices, I'd convince myself I was no longer attached to her every movement. Then she'd slip again, and I'd slide right down with her. I hated myself every time I did this.

"Pain is not always a bad thing," my therapist once told me. "Pain can motivate us toward positive change. It can create compassion and help us grow." Still, pain is not something a mother can easily tolerate when it comes to her children. Demeter had to learn a new way to relate to her daughter's trauma. I did, too.

Later that week, when I went to the coffee shop for my meeting with Mary, she was already standing in line waiting to order.

"Do you want anything?" she asked with a big smile.

"No. I'm too upset to eat," I said. At the table, Mary took her time removing her coat. She set down her coffee mug and muffin, then dug around in her oversized tote bag, searching for a notebook. I twitched, watching her.

"So, what's up?" Mary asked.

I launched into my non-stop recital of concerns. When I'd finished, I waited for her response. She took a slow bite of her muffin, then looked at me.

"What did you expect?" I heard Mary's question but couldn't speak right away. Instead, I twisted the napkin in my lap. We'd been working on the 12 Steps for a while. Our progress was slow, partly because I was dragging my feet on Step Four, the step that asks you to go beyond simply being aware of your shortcomings and take responsibility for changing your behavior.

"I thought she had resources," I said. "After so many months of rehab, AA meetings, and therapy, I thought she'd know how to keep herself on track."

"What about you? Has it been so easy for you to deal with your pain, the pain of her relapsing?" Mary was calm and compassionate, and irritatingly patient. I stared at her latte—the foam had flattened out.

"What do you mean?" My voice was childlike.

"You seem to be right back into your old habit of trying to get her well so you can feel better." The coffee shop suddenly felt too crowded, too noisy. I looked around the room, hoping to find a way out of this conversation. I couldn't use the "you-don't-know-what-it's-like-to-have-daughter-dealing-with-addiction" argument. Mary knew all too well.

"I'm just worried she will do something stupid or unintentional," I said. "You heard about Philip Seymour Hoffman overdosing earlier this year? So many people seem to be accidentally dying lately. That could happen to her."

"That's true, but you can't control Olivia's recovery," Mary said.

"I know the Al-Anon saying that I 'didn't cause, can't control, and can't cure' someone's addiction, but I can't just watch this happen again."

"You've already done what you can do to help Olivia," Mary said. I stared out the window. An oversized beer truck was backing up in the café parking lot. I couldn't look away until I was sure the driver wouldn't run over the curb.

"The question remains," she continued. "How are you going to recover?"

I didn't have an answer. I didn't want to have one. *Why do mothers have to be saints?* I wondered. I studied the sugar sprinkled around Mary's plate. Then I thought about Demeter. She didn't have to deal with someone telling her she was codependent or enabling. Instead, she raged and fought and demanded results. But even the rants of a goddess couldn't change the fact that Demeter's daughter had been captured and taken to Hell. At what point was Demeter willing to face that?

A month after her friend's death, Olivia was stumbling but heading in the right direction, bushwhacking a path through the brambles of her recovery. She couldn't keep working at the deli counter next to the ghost of a boy who'd once flirted with her, so she found a new job. She also found solace with a guy named Isaac, someone she'd met earlier at an AA meeting. He was fifteen years older than she. Isaac encouraged Olivia to get sober again, and their relationship was good for a while. Olivia told me how excited she was to be in love with a mature man. The age difference didn't matter to her, she said. I took Mary's advice and decided to "keep my mouth shut and my mind open."

It was early spring when I drove to Nashville. I'd invited Olivia to join me at an Airbnb for the weekend. The house we rented had whitewashed wood paneling inside and a retro-style red refrigerator. It reminded me of a beach cabin I'd visited when I was Olivia's age.

"This is so cute!" Olivia said when she walked in. I hugged her and took her overnight bag to one of the bedrooms.

"I know. Tonight, we can eat popcorn and watch a movie together.

"Perfect."

That evening, I stir-fried chicken and vegetables. Olivia made quinoa and salad. We kept the conversation light, talking about books and movies, her roommates, and her work. Snuggled next to each other on the couch after dinner, I massaged her feet and imagined we were on an island, just the two of us, as if the past several years hadn't happened.

The next day, the sun was shining. We decided to go on a picnic. Olivia was amazed that I'd found a park in the middle of Nashville, her new hometown. She was always awed at my maternal ability to investigate her surroundings no matter where she was. As we pulled into the tiny parking lot, the sun was climbing in the Tennessee sky, heating up the asphalt. I took off my sweater, and Olivia removed her flannel shirt. Standing in an orange tank top, she turned to reveal a new tattoo. It was an abstract image of a bull covering her right shoulder. Big and thickly black, it looked more like a Pacific Island tattoo, not lacey like the ones I was used to seeing in the South.

"Isn't it cool?" she asked. "It's me. Taurus. I designed it myself." I drew in a deep breath, hoping to swallow my tongue. All I could see was more graffiti permanently marked on the wall of my daughter's delicate flesh. Rather than wait for my reply, Olivia took off, walking ahead of me toward the park. I studied her strong limbs and watched her high chestnut ponytail bounce from side to side above her proud dancer's gate. She looked lovely and so much healthier than two years before.

I'll get used to the tattoo, I told myself.

Carrying a small backpack with water, turkey sandwiches, and two chocolate chip cookies, I followed her through the park's archway of pink rhododendrons. A warm spring breeze kicked up, and I caught a whiff of Olivia's perfume. Out of habit, I sniffed again, like a hound dog looking for clues. I noticed the angry burn scar on the back of her calf—the skin still buckled and red where the flames had torched her.

Olivia often chose to forget the drama she could no longer see, but I always had a ringside seat. Despite her recommitment to sobriety, she still lived in a haze, the residual effect of time spent numb from drugs and drifting in a dark underworld. Until she could see herself more clearly, I knew it was up to me to provide a mirror for her. As I followed her through the park, past a baseball field, and toward a stand of trees, I wondered, *Which vision of her will my fear allow me to hold?*

We meandered across railroad tracks, around a golf course, and toward a little river. A guy on a tractor was mowing near the freeway, releasing the green smell of fresh grass. At the wooden footbridge, we stopped to peer down at the water transporting twigs and pink blossoms under us.

Keeping her eyes on the river, Olivia began to sing in a soft voice:
"As I went down in the river to pray
Studying about that good old way
And who shall wear the starry crown
Good Lord, show me the way
O brother, let's go down…"

It was an old mountain song. Her singing was sweet and unexpected, so unlike anything she had said or done over the past twelve months. I almost cried. *Where did she learn this song?* Tentative at first, I joined her at the chorus. We never looked at each other. Leaning over the rough railing, side by side, we sang out and over the shallow, rippling water. We sang to the quiet maple and oak trees that lined the narrow river. We sang to the great blue heron stalking his lunch in the green shadows below us, deftly picking up one long leg, then the other.

We kept singing—two voices, tender and clear, sharing the same genes, the same longing. We sang a second verse: "O daughter, let's go down," then another: "O mother, won't you come on down." Olivia held her own beautifully. She sang a strong melody, maintaining her line as I harmonized. Verse after verse, we sang, unsure when to stop but trusting each other to know. When the last note faded to a hush, we spoke no words, exchanged no glances. Instead, we straightened up, crossed over the shady bridge, and walked into the noonday sun. She grabbed my hand.

DEMETER (RE-IMAGINED)
The Promise of Spring

In the winter, Demeter waited for her daughter's homecoming. She used those cold, quiet days to gather herself and practice sitting quietly rather than feeding her anxiety. Sometimes, she walked to the meadow where Persephone once played and studied the puffy clouds passing overhead. Each year, Demeter grew wiser, more patient—trusting. She became attuned to her surroundings, learning to anticipate the icy winds that blew from the north and relishing the magenta sunsets that glowed through leafless trees. Demeter could not help mourning her daughter's absence, but she found a way to be at peace with it.

Several days before Persephone's arrival, Demeter knew winter was over. There would be a warm, moist wind blowing from the south, bringing with it the fragrance of almond tree blossoms. Hares would begin making nests in the fields, and deer would retreat deeper into the woods to birth their young. Dew laced the hard ground each dawn, and tiny drops of water bejeweled spider webs in the trees. As the sun lifted over the mountain, all manner of birds began singing their overtures to new beginnings, while doves, the ancient symbol of love and fertility, cooed in the late afternoons.

In the distance, the figure of a young woman walked toward Demeter. Radiant as the sun, Persephone was the perpetual promise of spring. A beautiful wreath adorned her long curls, and her soft green robes matched the color of tender grass. Demeter smiled as she noticed flowers blooming with each footstep Persephone took. Soon, there would be paths of wildflowers covering the hillside.

The Ascent

Olivia and Isaac were together for several months. As her roller-coaster life headed for the next bend, I could see the warning signs she ignored. Isaac was a nice guy, but the more she talked about their future together, the more he distanced himself until he wasn't there at all.

She was upset about their breakup but tried to convince herself it was for the best. One evening, when she was getting ready to go to a recovery meeting, she decided to wear a new dress she'd bought. She put on makeup and her favorite earrings. After the meeting, she hung around outside smoking cigarettes with her friends. She was hoping to talk to Isaac, but he'd left early.

It was about 10 p.m. and raining by the time Olivia got to her car. She cried as she drove onto the dark highway and stopped at the first red light. When the light turned green, Olivia turned left. She never saw the car going full speed toward her in the oncoming lane. It smashed into her Prius on the passenger front corner. Everyone was fine except Olivia. Her airbag failed to inflate, and she'd neglected to buckle up. Her face went through the windshield, causing a nasty gash from her left forehead across her right eyebrow, just missing her eye. Her car was totaled.

An ambulance came, and several people from the recovery meeting across the street ran over to see what had happened. Someone called Isaac, and he met her at the emergency room. When we got the call from Olivia, it was close to midnight. Henri sat up in bed. I turned on the light while he put her on speakerphone so I could hear.

"Hi, Olivia. Is everything alright?" Henri asked.

"Yeah. So, Isaac said I have to call you." She sounded breathless, hurried.

"Where are you?"

"I'm in the emergency room in Nashville. There was an accident. But everyone is fine. I just wanted you to know."

Henri was asking her more questions. I was already in my closet, pulling out pants, a sweater, and underwear to throw in a bag.

"Another car hit me. There was broken glass and a lot of blood everywhere. A woman was screaming because she thought I was dead. I got a cut on my face, but the doctor stitched it up. I'm just waiting now to be released."

I asked Henri if a plastic surgeon would be doing the stitching. Then, I heard Olivia on the speaker say, "And, Dad, tell Mom NOT to come." I stopped packing, walked over to the phone, and leaned into it so I knew she would hear me.

"Are you sure, Olivia? I can be there soon. It's no problem."

"Mom, it's fine. Isaac said he could take me home." That's when I realized she was hoping she might get back with Isaac. The last thing she wanted was her mother there. Not knowing what to do with myself, I paced the bedroom floor, went to the kitchen to get a cup of tea, and returned to bed. I could sense Malvado standing nearby, chewing on an unlit cigarette, waiting for me to do something.

Sleep didn't come. I kept seeing Olivia alone in her car, covered in blood and glass, sirens wailing, black rain coming down, the cop asking if she'd been drinking, the kids from the recovery meeting convincing the cop that she was sober. I wanted to be there for her, wanted to be a good mother, but I was beginning to see that by not jumping into the car to drive to Nashville, I was giving her something she needed more: I was hearing her. Still, I recognized an old childhood pain of not feeling wanted or important creeping into my chest. I closed my eyes and put my hand on my heart, then took a few deep breaths to quiet my thoughts. In my mind, I willed Malvado to acknowledge this healthy shift and watched him back away toward the door to leave.

Olivia didn't relapse. Despite her headaches from the accident, despite her heartache about not getting back with Isaac, she didn't turn to drugs. She continued with recovery meetings and trained herself to wait—another hour, another day, another month—rather than succumb to the crushing desire for immediate relief. Thanks to the community of AA people in Nashville, Olivia found the strength and support she needed to stay sober. There was a blue crack in the grey sky.

Olivia managed to stay clean and sober for a year. She rented a room in a Nashville house full of creative and positive people, got a new job, and went to the gym regularly. The following Thanksgiving, Olivia looked great. Her skin had a healthy glow, her body looked more muscular, and she smiled a lot. She met with friends during the day but lingered with us over dinners, chatting about her life.

One evening, she asked Henri and me to sit with her in the living room. "I have an announcement to make," she said. In the past, Olivia's announcements ranged from "I'm dropping out of college," to "I'm a heroin addict," to "I'm in love with a thirty-seven-year-old man." She always threw us a curveball. Even if I wanted to try, I was afraid to guess what she would say. I held my breath.

"I've saved money from my job and have decided to walk the Appalachian Trail starting in March. I'd like to come home after Christmas and get ready for it—if that's alright."

"That's fantastic," Henri said. I agreed. We were thrilled that Olivia wanted to spend time outdoors and try something adventuresome.

"Hiking the Appalachian Trail is a huge undertaking," a friend later told me one afternoon while we were on a walk. "It starts in Georgia and goes 2,190 miles to Maine."

"How long does it take to hike all that way?" I asked.

"Like five to seven months," she said. "And you have to climb up to 6,000 feet at one point. Half the hikers who start it don't go more than a quarter of the way. It's too hard."

I went home and told Henri what my friend had said. Even though the Appalachian Trail passes near Asheville, Henri and I knew next to nothing about the hike.

"That sounds like a lot. Plus, she'll be leaving in March," he said. "She'll probably wake up to snow more than once."

"I'm happy that she wants to challenge herself, and it's great that she wants to do something outdoors, but Olivia has never been on a hiking trip. She's only slept in a tent a few times in her life," I said. "She has scoliosis and will carry a heavy pack for hours at a time, day after day. How is this going to work?"

"I don't know," Henri said. "Hopefully, she'll last a week or two. It'll be worth it for her to try something new. She'll be fine."

A few days later, I knocked on Olivia's bedroom door. After small talk, I asked how she would prepare for her trek. She rolled her eyes, shrugged her shoulders, said she'd "figure it out," and then left the room. Olivia was over twenty-one years old, but at that moment, we were both transported back to her high school years. I translated her comment to mean she would borrow someone's leaky tent, find the old sleeping bag she used in middle school for slumber parties, and toss a few power bars in her pocket. That exchange was all it took for me to assume she was not mature enough to handle this journey. I went downstairs, opened my computer, and began educating myself about the Appalachian Trail.

I read about hypothermia, dehydration, people getting lost, snakes, and bear attacks. One article talked about local hunters who liked to prey on young girls hiking alone. The more I learned about all the things that could go wrong, the more my eyes bore into my computer screen. I researched what and how much hikers need to eat and downloaded a detailed map of the route, taping the map to our refrigerator and marking the spots where I could send drop boxes of food and supplies along the way. Next, I checked consumer report ratings then selected (and paid for) the optimal tent, poles, backpack, sleeping bag, and raingear.

Commandeering our upstairs den, I dubbed it "Operation AT." Carefully laying out hiking clothes in one pile, I made another pile that included a tiny first-aid kit, flashlight, extra batteries, sunscreen, a laundry line, and a miniature Swiss army knife. I put two weeks' worth of dry breakfasts, lunches, and dinners into individual zip bags. I assembled and then re-assembled Olivia's pack, trying to make it lighter. At one point, Olivia found me on the floor, filing a toothbrush in half so it would weigh less.

"What are you doing, Mom?"

"Oh, nothing," I said, sawing harder to make the toothbrush hurry up and break.

"I appreciate all this, but you don't have to do it," she said.

"Once you're on the trail, you'll be on your own. I just want to make sure you don't freeze or starve the first week." I tried to make it sound like a joke. "Anyway, I'm having fun." That's when I knew I was in full relapse mode, out of control. I caught a glimpse of Malvado, his long brown coat flapping as he paced around the room, shaking his head in disgust.

Okay, okay, I know, I said to him in my mind. *Now, go away.* Lately, I'd come to see Malvado as a messenger more than a demon. He'd often appear not to torture me but to remind me what I still had to learn. But this time felt different. I was embarrassed that I'd fallen so far behind in my recovery. I wanted him to disappear.

Why am I doing all this? I wondered. Caught in the same loop, the same desire to make sure my daughter would be safe, it seemed I'd failed to learn anything about my own addictions. I put down the toothbrush, sat back, and cried. There was a piece missing in my understanding of myself, something I couldn't seem to access. *Why am I so afraid Olivia might die?* This question haunted me more than my mother's judgments. But then, I remembered the many losses Henri and I suffered before Olivia was born. No matter how hard I tried to protect my daughter, I knew from experience that there were no guarantees in life.

Part Four

Old Sorrows

About a year after we married, Henri and I moved to Brooklyn. We were both in our early thirties. He was entering his fellowship at Columbia University's medical center in Manhattan, and I had a new job at the Brooklyn Academy of Music. Our apartment was at the top of a slender three-floor walk-up in the Cobble Hill neighborhood. It had a bedroom barely big enough for the bed and a tiny kitchen squeezed into a space that once was a closet. We loved our new home and decided we were ready to start a family. I soon became pregnant and immediately began daydreaming about being a mother.

In the 1980s, this part of Brooklyn was still heavily Italian. Grandmothers in their aprons and headscarves monitored the day's activities from their upstairs windowsills. After midnight, a collective hush quieted the streets as the neighborhood slumbered. In the middle of one of those silent nights, I started cramping. I knew this wasn't my period—the pregnancy test I'd taken clearly displayed a positive blue line. My groans woke Henri. I was doubled over on the bed, sweating and unable to speak. Henri grabbed his shiny new doctor bag, pulled out a blood pressure cuff, and began wrapping it around my arm. I could see his hand shaking as he tried to locate my pulse.

"I think I'm going to be sick," I said, swatting away his stethoscope and lurching to the bathroom. I felt lightheaded. The room started listing to one side. I tried to grab the sink to right myself but fell to my knees. I wanted to lie down and put my face on the cold tile, but my stomach cramps started up again. As soon as I hoisted myself onto the toilet, I heard a plop then saw what looked like a large blood clot. I had expelled the dream of my baby into a bowl of wastewater.

At the clinic the next day, a doctor confirmed that I had miscarried. I tried to think of Amelia Earhart skimming too close to a set of palm trees while attempting her first solo landing, then swooping back up into the air again.

I'll do better next time, I told myself.

We moved to Asheville a year later. When a bold blue line appeared again on a pregnancy test kit, I was more cautious this time and waited before telling my news to the world. By three months, my body was beginning to recognize its new inhabitant. My breasts were tender, and I had to carry around a box of saltines in my car to keep from getting sick. I wondered if I was having a boy or a girl.

"Let's see how things are going," my doctor said at our check-up as he readied me for the ultrasound exam. He was about my age, a tall guy with dark hair and tan skin from a summer's worth of golf games. Henri and I were excited—we were going to hear the baby's heartbeat for the first time. The exam should have been routine. It should have been fine. The doctor made a pass or two around my belly then stopped and shook his head. He looked like he was going to cry. You could tell this was the part of obstetrics that he hated, the part no one warned him about in medical school.

"I'm so sorry," he said. "There isn't a heartbeat. It's too late today to do a D&C, but I will schedule one for you first thing in the morning." He left us alone in the examining room to stare at each other and hold hands. I was too stunned to cry. I spent the next seventeen hours walking around, eating dinner, and trying to sleep with something dead inside me before going into the hospital to have all remnants of motherhood scraped away.

This miscarriage didn't feel like a false landing. It felt like I'd crashed hard on the ground without warning. I was broken in spirit, emptied of meaning. I collected all my thoughts about cute baby clothes and names to consider, packed everything into a mental box, and bolted the lid. Henri and I planted a tree in the backyard to have something alive to watch grow, but I couldn't help imagining my child growing up along with it.

The following summer, after a frustrating year of trying, I finally became pregnant again. I was thrilled when we passed the first trimester without incident, but my doctor recommended that I quit my consulting work with a local ad agency and stay at home to take it easy. I was happy to comply, ready to do anything to have a healthy birth.

At five-months pregnant, I woke up one night to go to the bathroom and felt a gush of fluid pour from inside me into the toilet. I walked to the bedroom and flipped on the overhead light to wake Henri. "My water broke too early. It's over," I announced. Henri bolted up from sleep, stood naked by his side of the bed for a moment then started pulling on his pants. I'd never seen him move that fast.

"You don't know that," he said. "Get dressed. We're going to the hospital right now."

"It's over," I whispered.

We raced to the hospital, and a nurse immediately took me to a room. My doctor arrived to examine me. Someone was talking on the phone down the hall, but otherwise, the unit was dead quiet. I noticed I was breathing in the stale smell of a hospital after it had labored all day with emergencies and before the morning cleaning crew arrived.

"I'm sorry, but this fetus can't survive now," the doctor said. I'd already prepared myself for the worst, but Henri's eyes became fixed, his body wooden.

"Will you do a D&C?" I asked.

"No. I'll give you something that will help induce labor."

I didn't realize I would have to deliver a child who would never live. There would be no Lamaze classes, no perineal massage, no epidural, no baby announcements. After months of bedrest, there would be nothing to show for my efforts, only empty arms to take home. The doctor turned the lights down in the room, and we waited for my contractions to begin.

The pain came on fast. I felt something searing and then ripping. It was as if a battle was raging inside me—the drugs trying to eliminate a foreign element, and my body refusing to let go. I was trying not to scream but couldn't help gasping and crying. Then, suddenly, the pain, and the birth, was over.

"It's a boy," the doctor said after a nurse cleaned our baby and wrapped him in a blue and pink striped receiving blanket. "He probably died coming through the birth canal. Do you want to hold him?"

"No!" we both said.

"In my experience, women who have stillbirths often do better if they hold their baby. It can help with the grief process," the doctor said.

Henri and I were both crying. We were still unsure, but then I reached for our son. He was surprisingly heavy in my arms. I looked at his tiny face, his straight black hair, his eyes closed shut. Our boy was beautiful—almost too beautiful.

Then, something happened so quickly that I didn't have time to wonder if I was crazy. A bright light engulfed the room. In front of me, I saw a path with a row of trees on either side. A white fire, shimmering and brilliant, consumed the trees. Even more uncanny was this: despite my tears, for a brief instance, I also felt blissful, as if I could feel myself smiling inside. Then everything went back to being an ordinary hospital room again.

I remember thinking, *If such deep sorrow and complete joy can exist at the same moment, there must be a God.* I didn't know if that was God or me speaking. I didn't know if I imagined this experience or if it was some kind of epiphany. But I did know it had something to do with birthing our baby, with me being a mother, with what was to come. I didn't tell Henri. It seemed too strange to admit to anyone.

Every morning for a week after I got home, I cried in the shower as I watched useless milk leak from my breasts onto the tile floor and disappear down the drain. A mailman delivered a new copy of *American Baby* magazine to my house. The issue focused on "the joys of having a newborn." The second issue arrived a month later. That cover announced: "Now Your Baby is One Month Old!" This was part of a marketing campaign, I realized. They mailed the magazine to every pregnant woman who came into the hospital, whether she wanted it or not. About the time I'd stopped crying every day, an official death certificate arrived in the mail from the hospital with my son's tiny footprints on a notecard. Above the print, it simply said, "Baby Boy."

So, he had been real after all, I thought.

Months after the stillbirth, I'd find myself driving to do an errand, stopping my car in a parking lot, and sitting catatonic behind the wheel for thirty minutes—or maybe it was an hour. I couldn't tell. One morning,

I remember sitting on the side of my bed staring out the window. I had a kitchen knife in my hand. It wasn't very sharp, but I held it against my wrist thinking it didn't matter if I was alive or dead.

———————————

For years, I secretly tortured myself, worrying that I was to blame for my pregnancy failures. *Maybe I moved around too much or didn't eat the right things. If only I had a body made to carry these children to term, maybe they wouldn't have had to die.* My "unmoorings," I called them—little spirits whose mother couldn't manage to give them a sure footing on dry land. They had suffered enough. I would carry the weight of regret for them—it was the least I could do.

Regret became a temporary solution to a long-term problem. It kept me focused on all that went wrong, all that could have been, and all that was lost. If I immersed myself in regret, I could ignore the fear at the bottom of my heart, the secret that I might still be inadequate. Once I gave birth to Austin and Olivia, I promised myself I would do everything in my power to be the best mother for them. But it never felt like enough. When it was clear Olivia was struggling with bulimia in high school, and then later, in college, when she became addicted to heroin, I held myself in contempt, an emotional debtors' prison. I became a junkie for regret.

DEMETER (RE-IMAGINED)
Her Daughter's Destiny

Once Demeter accepted her daughter as a powerful and capable woman, a queen of her own universe, she began to see things in a new light. Each spring, she created a world bursting with color and sweet smells to celebrate her daughter's return and as a tribute to all Persephone had accomplished through her trials and triumphs. By allowing Persephone to live for a time each year in the Underworld, Demeter also encouraged her daughter to transform those experiences into something of beauty, meaning, and purpose.

The only god to have a dual role, Persephone was the Goddess of Fertility on Earth and Queen of the Dead in the Underworld. She was often depicted holding sheaves of grain in one hand and a burning torch in the other. Her experience in the Underworld uniquely qualified her to instruct others about the process of death, recovery, and renewal, guiding them through the fearful transition from one world to the next. Had she not traveled through the fires of her abduction, she would have forgone her true purpose.

Seasons of Recovery

Olivia plugged her music into the car radio and chose an oldies playlist so we both could sing along. We drove south for three hours, snaking through the Blue Ridge Mountains toward the place in Georgia where the Appalachian Trail begins. Green highway signs announced the names of towns I recognized from staring at the AT map. Olivia would soon be hiking up and over these same mountain ranges.

It seemed fitting that she chose the AT for her walkabout rather than the Pacific Crest Trail or the Continental Divide Trail. In the 1800s, her ancestors, my mother's people, once laid down roots on a rolling mountain plateau called Ashe County in Western North Carolina. The county's main river is called the New River, but it's one of the oldest rivers in the world. During the nineteenth and early twentieth centuries, this area was referred to as a "lost province" because it was so isolated. *A good place to find oneself,* I remember thinking. I still have my great-great-grandmother's crazy quilt, its splintered bits of brightly colored silks and velvets intricately stitched onto a black background. A photograph of her shows a tall woman, looking stately and proud. I imagined her encouraging Olivia along the hike, whispering to her through the maples, oaks, sourwoods, and pines.

Olivia was quiet as we drove. I looked at her hand fiddling with the radio knobs. I remember noticing her hands on the day she was born, thinking how easy it would be for her to reach an octave on the piano with her long fingers. Her hands are slender, lovely—not short and square like mine. They are also surprisingly strong. When she was young, she was ticklish, and I used to grab her knee while she sat next to me in the car.

It always made her jump, and she would laugh. But once, I did it when she was in a bad mood, and she clenched down on my hand, painfully twisting it away. I was more careful not to cross her after that. As we drove toward Georgia, I reached over to hold her hand. It felt warm and soft, and she didn't pull away for a very long time.

I'd made a reservation for us to spend the night at the Amicalola Falls Lodge, a popular spot for hikers that felt more like a hostel than a hotel. We dropped our bags in our room and went to the restaurant for dinner, choosing a table for two. Once seated, I turned to look out the tall, cold window next to us, but there was nothing to see—no moon or stars or city lights, only a black canvas.

I thought about the night before we left Asheville when Olivia and I sat on our living room rug together in front of the fire. "I'm not worried about the physical part of the hike," she'd said as a tear rolled down her cheek. "But what if I'm lonely?" I tried to be reassuring, but I could feel my shoulders tighten.

A waiter came, and I ordered red wine. Olivia asked for a diet Coke, and I immediately felt embarrassed. At first, I told myself I needed the wine to calm my nerves, but all I had to do the next day was drive Olivia into the woods, wish her well, then get in my warm car and drive back to Asheville. *How can I expect her to stay sober when I can't stop myself from ordering a glass of wine?*

We woke up early the following day to drive to the trailhead. The dirt road was steep and winding. The higher we climbed, the closer we came to cold, wintery clouds hanging just above the barren trees. At the end of the road was a small parking lot about a mile into the Appalachian Trail.

"I can't start here," Olivia said. "I have to go to the beginning."

"Okay, I'll hike back with you."

We took off together, bundled against the cold, the wind making our noses red and runny as we walked. I couldn't imagine myself hiking to Maine. The official AT marker was just a plaque on a rock. I took some photos to record the moment, and then we retraced our steps to the parking lot. At the car, I gave Olivia one last hug.

"I'll help you put on your pack," I said. The pack was bright orange—a color we agreed would help hunters not mistake her for a deer—and it was heavy, laden with all the stuff I convinced her she would need to stay warm, hydrated, and safe. I had to bend my knees to lift it out of the trunk and then hoist it onto her shoulders. She buckled the waist strap, turned around, and started up the hill. The forest was empty, silent. Even the birds seemed to have disappeared. I stood by the car, watching her walk away, a Gretel without Hansel. She looked so young and inexperienced. I felt like the wicked stepmother.

"Leave a trail of breadcrumbs," I yelled as she headed up the hill. Her pack was too heavy for her to twist around, but she gave a thumbs up over her head and kept going. Soon, she was out of sight.

When I got in my car, I teared up and had trouble focusing on the gravel lane down the mountain. Once I got to the highway, I was clear-eyed but still concerned. As I drove, I thought about Olivia sleeping the first of many nights on some hillside in the forest. Would she put her tent up too soon and be bored and cold for hours, or would she wait until dusk and then have to fumble around in the dark? Would the food she carried be enough to sustain her? Would she get lost, be bitten by snakes, or attacked by rednecks? Despite my mind's obsessiveness, I could also feel my heart overflowing with enormous pride. My daughter, if anything, was brave.

The ring of my cell phone jolted me out of those musings. I was surprised to see it was Olivia.

"Hey, sweetie!"

"Hi, Mom." Just hearing those two words, I could tell she was about to cry.

"What's up?"

"I don't know. I'm sad. I don't think I can do this." It took all my strength to keep the car heading home and not turn around to pick her up.

"Well, honey, I'm halfway home." This was a lie. I could hear her crying. "Open your pack. I put a tiny red notebook in there for times like this. Read that, then text me later and let me know how you're doing. You're going to be fine."

"Okay," she said and hung up.

Before she'd left, I spent a couple of weeks looking for encouraging quotes and writing them into this notebook. If I couldn't be there, I wanted a holy host of angels, poets, philosophers, and wise ones to accompany her. I titled it the *Hiker's Little Book*—a takeoff on the AA Big Book. It included sayings from other hikers ("The best way to carry water is inside you," and "Always pack your sense of humor."); John Muir ("Going to the mountains is going home."); Jack Kerouac; Sir Edmund Hillary; Longfellow ("The best thing one can do when it rains is let it rain."); C.S. Lewis; Thoreau ("I took a walk into the woods and came out taller than the trees."); Dickens ("I have been bent and broken, but, I hope, into a better shape."); Moliere; Lord Byron; Cheryl Strayed; Albert Einstein ("Look deep into nature, and then you will understand everything better."); Van Gogh; Willa Cather ("There are some things you learn best in calm, others in storm."); Langston Hughes; Walt Whitman. There were quotes by Churchill and Eleanor Roosevelt, Mother Teresa and Andy Warhol, Ram Dass and Oscar Wilde. I copied sayings from AA like "one day at a time" and "start a gratitude list." There were Zen proverbs, Japanese proverbs, African proverbs. I added a few messages from me about the hero's journey, and how every day is a clean slate. And at the end, I added things I'd remembered Olivia saying ("If I can be clean and sober for a year, I know I can do anything").

Two hours later, she sent a text: "Thanks, Mom."

Olivia was not afraid to walk into the wilderness alone. I was enormously proud of my daughter, but I still wanted her to be more like me. I had a fantasy that once on the Appalachian Trail, Olivia would fall in with a group of fresh-faced kids who looked like they'd stepped out of an REI catalog. How little I understood about hiking the AT, or about Olivia, for that matter. Olivia was edgier than I ever was, and she gravitated toward people who could appreciate her struggles in life. I knew the more I could accept our differences, the less she would feel judged by me. Now that she was beginning to trust herself, it was time for me to trust her, too. This was the next step in my recovery.

The first photos Olivia sent us via text from the AT showed a bedraggled group of her new friends huddled in makeshift tents. The people who stay on the trail for months at a time lovingly call themselves "hiker trash." After a while, they become like feral children—dirty, smelly, laughing, and singing. They walk through God's country in a perpetual state of presence, thinking only about getting to the next destination. Comforted each day by the sun's warmth and delighted each night by the stars, they follow a hiker code of conduct and bond like a family, sharing their food, stories, and dreams.

After two weeks hiking through the Blue Ridge Mountains, Olivia told us she'd be passing near Asheville. I drove to meet her at River's End Restaurant in the Nantahala Gorge, a place where the Appalachian Trail briefly dips into civilization before zigzagging back into the hills. A handful of other young hikers came with her, and I bought them all breakfast. They giggled, made fun of each other, and swooned over the eggs and pancakes. Olivia seemed totally at ease. Her cheeks were slightly sunburned, her shoulders looked broader, and when she smiled, it was as if the sun had finally burst through the clouds. She was happier than I'd ever seen her.

It took Olivia three months to trudge her way over 800 miles through Georgia, North Carolina, and Virginia. At one point, she decided to hike ahead of her friends and spend some time alone, but a bad thunderstorm made her stop. It rained so hard she was stuck in her tent for two days. Her phone battery died, so she couldn't read any downloaded books. There was nothing to do for hours except listen to the rain, stare at the nylon ceiling of her tent, and try not to notice the water pooling around her sleeping bag. On the third day, bored and restless, she waited for a break in the rain, packed her wet gear, and took off on the trail again. It was late in the afternoon when she came to a clearing on the mountain. Threatening thunderclouds formed overhead as cold rain began to pelt her. Not wanting to be in an open field during a storm, she tried to scurry toward the woods for cover, but a massive bolt of fiery lightning struck the ground next to her.

"I screamed like a little girl and ran five miles back to the campsite," she later told me. "The pack was so heavy! By then, it was dark, and I was stumbling and falling a lot, but I was so scared I kept going."

Once at the site, she set up her tent, crawled inside, and waited for daylight. In the morning, she could barely move. She called me in tears saying the pain in her back was excruciating.

"Get to the nearest road and wait for me at a gas station," I said. "I'll leave right now." I drove five hours to Virginia to pick her up, turned around, and brought her home. Even after resting for a week and seeing her chiropractor, Olivia could not rejoin her friends and finish the

Appalachian Trail. Her back was a mess.

I hoped Olivia could be proud of her time hiking the AT. Instead, she fell into a deep depression for months. This is not uncommon. Many hikers have difficulty leaving behind the magic and camaraderie found on the trail. But with Olivia, it was more than that. She felt like a failure for having to quit early. She thought she'd be hiking until October. With the passing weeks, she imagined how each section of the trail might look from Virginia to Maine. Late in the summer, I found her sitting on our deck one day, staring at the mountains and clutching her cell phone.

"They're not texting me," she said.

"I suspect your trail friends are out of range," I said.

"Yeah, having the time of their lives."

Olivia got a job at a restaurant in Asheville, rented a room in a house with two guys she didn't know, and waited for her life to begin again. Her body was fit from climbing mountains, but she seemed emotionally exhausted.

"What you did was truly amazing," I said. "We're so proud of you. I don't know anyone who could have hiked that long."

"You don't know my friends. They'll all make it to Maine except me."

"But you didn't give up. You hurt your back."

"I can never do anything, Mom. What's wrong with me?" I sat back and peered at her as if looking into a mirror. I was self-punishing in a similar way, unwilling to acknowledge all the healthy mothering skills I'd acquired over the past several years. Instead, I downplayed the love, care, and attention I'd given my children, refusing to let myself off the hook. For all the work I'd done on myself, I was still focusing on the times I'd slipped backwards. Yet, part of me realized that each time I recovered, I was a little wiser, a little healthier.

Recovery is not something that happens once. It begins when someone ends substance abuse or other unhealthy behaviors and then works toward creating a more positive lifestyle and mindset over time. Long-term recovery evolves in cycles the way chord progressions build in a musical piece or trees expand with growth rings. Each winter, when a tree seems to die, it sends stronger roots into the Earth to emerge more robust in the spring.

When Olivia was at rehab and Henri and I came for the family weekend, a counselor had asked us what our wishes were for each other. Olivia said her wish for me was that I take care of myself. I assumed then that she simply didn't want to be weighed down by my sadness regarding her addiction. I'd done my best to be a good mother, or at least be more attentive and emotionally open than my mother was to me. It wasn't until later that I understood I had to give her something more fundamental. If I was truly going to ease her suffering, I had to help her trust herself more and need me less. I remembered a conversation I'd recently had with Mary while we were walking around a lake in Asheville.

"If you want to evolve as the mother of an adult child in recovery," she'd said, "you have to change your relationship to motherhood."

"What does that mean, exactly? What am I supposed to do different-ly?" I was beginning to feel exasperated again as if nothing I did was ever enough.

"For starters, stop treating her like a victim. Her path may not be the one you would have chosen for her—but it might be better. Now that she's past active addiction, decide that she'll be okay."

"But I am already so proud of her, considering all her trauma. She's my hero."

"Do you see that even saying that assumes her trials are greater than other people's? Her life might be more dramatic than some, but every-one has challenges to overcome at some point in their lives. She's not unique. She will fall, but she'll pick herself up again like she's done so many times before. It's up to her now to build her self-worth."

"Then what am I supposed to do?"

"You have to let go of the old way of mothering. Instead, treat her like an adult. Let her see how you manage to grow in your life. Rather than a cheerleader or a coach, you can simply be a role model for her."

That evening, before bed, I quietly slid open the heavy glass door to our deck and slipped into the hot tub. The water felt warm and comforting against the snap of cold in the air. I loved being outside while the world slumbered. I could stay in the tub for twenty minutes or all night if I wanted. My time was my own. Looking up at the moonless sky, I found Orion's Belt and a faint trail of the Milky Way. Like the Ancient Greek mariners, I began using the stars to draw a picture in my mind—a sparkling sailboat racing across the heavens. *I can't pretend to sail Olivia's boat for her, but I have shown her the way,* I remember thinking. *Now, she'll have the stars to guide her, and I will always be here if she needs me.*

I thought about what had helped me cope over the past several years. At my lowest points, I'd always turned to journaling. Through writing, I could be honest about my insecurities, but I could also be reflective as if I were an observer. That process of self-discovery, seeing my life from a new perspective, helped me challenge my reactions. But it was not until I read the story of Demeter and Persephone that I began to relax.

How many mothers over the centuries learned from that myth? And how many other mothers, willing to honestly share their stories, released their daughters from negative patterns? Using my voice would help Olivia find hers. *But what story of myself do I want to give Olivia?* I wondered. The more I considered this question, my writing began to change. Rather than focusing on what had happened to my daughter, I started wondering what had happened to me. I didn't realize it at first, but keeping a journal morphed into writing a memoir.

Phase Two

"We're off!" Olivia said. This time, there was a plan. She was leaving for California to stay with a friend she'd met on the Appalachian Trail. He'd flown to Asheville to help her drive west to Sacramento, where she could look for a job.

The air was crisp and dry. The leaves were already orange and starting to fall. Olivia wanted to get an early start. After breakfast, she stuffed her car with bags of clothes and boxes of books and art supplies, things she would need to start over—again. I was standing barefoot on the gravel, still wearing my robe, watching her going in and out of the house. All I could see was the shadow of her face surrounded by a golden halo, her long soft curls down and sunlit from behind.

Godspeed, I thought.

Henri came out of the kitchen carrying a small cooler filled with sandwiches and seltzer and put it in the backseat. He gave Olivia a big hug, lifting her off the ground. Then, it was my turn.

"Have a great trip!" I said and hugged her tight. "Call us when you get there." I tried to sound breezy, tried not to cry. She promised to come home for a visit in April, and I was already imagining our reunion.

Olivia arranged a pillow in the passenger seat so her back wouldn't hurt, flashed a smile, and waved goodbye. I watched as they drove out of view and listened as the music from her car faded down the hill until it merged into the traffic noise below. The silence dug a hole in my chest. I didn't just miss her—I felt voided.

I thought of all the years I'd missed while she was in high school and college, all the mother–daughter times we didn't have because she was in active addiction of one kind or another. I thought about the long hikes we never took and the longer nights I lay awake worrying. I thought about how we dreamed of spending a weekend together in New York so we could visit galleries in Chelsea, shop in Soho, catch an off-Broadway play. But even when she lived in Asheville, we rarely went out together for lunch or coffee. For years, she was either high or busy avoiding me.

I wanted so desperately to have a close relationship with my daughter, one more intimate than my relationship with my mother. It wasn't that I didn't love my mother—I adored her, but her conversations with me were often superficial, and her unspoken needs were too deep. Whenever we were together, I felt like I was standing on the edge of the Grand Canyon. I'd have to shout and then wait for the wind to bounce my echo over to her. My mother would be standing on the other side. She couldn't catch what I was trying to say or didn't want to.

With Olivia, it was a little different. She chose to stay on her side of the canyon through adolescence, then the secrets, shame, and tyranny of drug abuse kept her there much longer. But when she went to rehab and started working the 12 Steps, and I later did the 12 Steps through Al-Anon, we grew closer. Rather than blindly accepting a distorted version of perfect womanhood handed down through generations, we were challenged to discover who we truly were. After several months, Olivia and I started sharing what we had learned. I was more open about my difficulties growing up. I also expressed how much I appreciated her and spoke up when I felt she wasn't treating me fairly. She began to do the same. As I learned to be vulnerable and honest, my role as her mother naturally changed. Although I still missed those lost years with Olivia, in many ways, our relationship became deeper than I could have imagined. We were finally on the same side of the canyon.

Standing in the driveway, I took a deep breath and pulled my fleece robe tighter around my neck. I climbed the stairs to Olivia's room, sat on her bed, and stared at her wall. There were photos from high school, drawings she'd done in middle school, concert ticket stubs, and ribbons from her days on the crew team tacked all around the room. She couldn't be bothered to go to the store and buy painter's tape to protect the walls. Instead, she'd used a staple gun to punch each memento into place. I smiled at the shiny silver staples positioned at odd angles in the sheetrock. Back when different things mattered to me, I might have been annoyed.

A week after Olivia left for California, I decided it was time for me to regroup. I dedicated a day to tackling my study, a small room large enough for a built-in desk and shelves that reached to the ceiling. This is where I dumped the details of my life that I didn't have time to deal with, or hoped to get back to, or wanted to ignore. On one side of my desk sat two unread novels, insurance forms that needed filing, several receipts, and old birthday cards. As I began sifting through the scattered parts of my life, I found a thick folder with articles about recovery and a pile of addiction self-help books I'd once carefully read and underlined. At the bottom of the stack was Tommy Rosen's book, *Recovery 2.0: Move Beyond Addiction and Upgrade Your Life*. I sat on the floor, flipped to the first chapter, and read for over an hour, nodding my head as I turned each page.

I'd met Tommy four years earlier at Kripalu, a yoga retreat center in western Massachusetts. It was spring 2014. Olivia was just out of rehab and working in Nashville. I'd gone to Kripalu with a friend for the weekend. On the first day of our retreat, my friend attended an early morning yoga session while I stopped in the cafeteria for breakfast before joining my watercolor workshop. After filling a plate with berries, a scone, and a tofu concoction resembling eggs, I looked for a place to sit down. Standing in the middle of the dining room, my tray in hand, I felt like a high schooler. No one looked up to acknowledge me. *How pompous they are,* I remember thinking, *dressed in their tank tops and yoga pants, like they're too enlightened to say hello*. I ate alone by the window, pretending to think deep thoughts as I looked out over a grassy knoll.

After my morning class, I had an hour to kill before lunch. Down the hall, there was some sort of open lecture happening. Everyone was sitting cross-legged on the floor in a circle. A stately, tall woman was telling her story. I stood at the entrance to the room to listen.

"I was an addict. And I was a sex worker," she said. "I reached my bottom and got sober, went to AA meetings, then returned to school to get an MBA. I stayed clean for eight years until I had a relapse. For me, the

12-Step program wasn't enough, so I stopped going to meetings and started doing yoga, which really helped. I was sober for five years, then relapsed again. But I finally found what worked." She scanned the silent faces. No one was breathing. We were all waiting to hear her next words. "I discovered it was the combination of yoga and the 12-Step program that kept me in long-term recovery. I needed them both." She talked about her recovery from co-dependence as a call to a new way of life. "If you can nurture yourself first," she said, "you'll have more than enough to nurture others."

I wanted to know more about this incredible woman but was too embarrassed to join the group late. The sign on the door read, "Kripalu Talk: Yoga and Recovery with Nikki Myers." There was also an announcement that a documentary called *The Anonymous People* would be screened that evening. Attitudes about addiction were beginning to change, the notice said: *Just like women with breast cancer, or people with HIV/ AIDS, courageous addiction recovery advocates are starting to come out of the shadows to tell their true stories.* I had no idea when I arrived at Kripalu that a recovery conference was happening the same weekend.

"You interested?" said a man standing behind me.

"Not for me. My daughter. She's just out of rehab."

"Tricky time. You should tell her to go online and check out the annual recovery conference. We're just starting it, and it's free to anyone."

"We?" I asked. The man in front of me had a huge smile. He looked healthy, fit, happy—not strained and broken after years of hard living, the way I'd imagined most ex-addicts looked.

"That's me," he said and pointed to the bulletin board. There was a poster of presenters for the recovery conference, including his picture and name: Tommy Rosen. That evening, I went to the film presentation and ran into Tommy again.

"Can I ask a question? I looked on your website, *Recovery 2.0*. What does that mean?"

"It means there are two phases to recovery. The first one is just getting to a 12-Step meeting, admitting there's a problem, and working on getting clean and sober. But most people stop there. They think that's all they need to do to stay in long-term recovery. Recovery 2.0 is the next phase."

This struck me as revolutionary. It was a given that many people returned to rehab again and again. Clearly, something wasn't working.

"You're saying it's not enough to stop the substance abuse and addictive behavior?"

"I'm saying it goes beyond even stopping addictive thinking. Recovery 2.0 is about addressing expectations, but it's also about examining our relationship to things like movement and food—it's a way to heal the body, mind, and spirit through a total lifestyle change. A new source of relief must be established as well as a regular practice of positive habits. Otherwise, it's too easy to slip back into the void."

"So, Recovery 2.0 is just for people in addiction?"

"It's for everyone, because we are all addicted to something one way or another." I hadn't considered that the emptiness Olivia experienced was an exaggeration of what everyone feels. I realized we weren't so dissimilar after all. Only our assumptions keep us apart.

I walked down to the cafeteria for lunch and was amazed at how warm and welcoming everyone was. Several people said hello, and a group of young yogis scooted over to make room for me at their table. I was pleased that the lunch crowd was nicer than the one at breakfast. As I left to return to my room, I noticed a sign in the hallway: "Silent Breakfast: Please do not talk."

For All the Joys
and Challenges

Oscar Wilde wrote, "We are all in the gutter, but some of us are looking at the stars." It's not a matter of us versus them—healthy people versus unhealthy, "normal" people versus those who are more challenged. Addiction, I had come to understand, is a hunger of the soul, a disconnect with the natural flow of life. The terror of loneliness, the tyranny of expectations, the fear that something is wrong with us, and the loss of faith. All this feeds into the desire for escape, the need to lessen the pain. I, too, had a hunger—a confusion and longing within me—and I was trying to fill it by thinking I could be the perfect mom.

With my daughter in long-term recovery, I should have been happy—or so I thought. Olivia was resilient and strong. She'd valiantly worked her way out of serious drug abuse and was now learning to face her challenges related to self-image and confidence. Periodically, she got sucked under by addictive thoughts or behavior, but the more I saw her reemerge, the more I trusted her process. Even so, I couldn't help feeling sad that she wasn't happy all the time. I was still waiting for everything to be all better, still worrying that something was wrong, and still linking my happiness to hers. Like Demeter, I was craving spring, a time when my daughter would return trouble-free.

Happiness is not the goal, Pema Chödrön writes. Allowing is the goal. With allowing comes contentment. I harbored expectations instead. First, my children had to be fine; second, I had to be a perfect mother; and third, life had to feel settled at some point.

But life is never settled, Pema says. Like the rivers, the forests, or the seasons, life always involves change—beginnings, endings, and beginnings again. These changes teach us and help us transform. To resist change only causes suffering.

In Yann Martel's book *Life of Pi*, there is a scene in which the hero, Pi, is drifting in the ocean in a little boat with a tiger. They are both hungry, thirsty, and exhausted, knowing they might die at any moment. Pi looks in the sky as if to address God. I expected him to lament, be angry, or beg for help. What he says instead touched my heart. And it's something that I say to myself every night when I look at the stars before I go to bed: "Thank you for my life."

Tommy Rosen says something similar at the end of his meditations. He says, "Thank you for the joys and challenges of my life." He doesn't say "Thank you for my blessings," as if God somehow grants our wishes or punishes our wrongdoings. Just simply thank you—for the opportunity to learn and grow, to practice living in alignment with the flow of life and reduce our own suffering.

Had the dual diseases of depression and addiction not taken hold of my daughter, I probably would have managed to get through life thinking our family was fine, much the same way my parents ignored the loneliness, hurt, and confusion happening within our home. Olivia's addiction made me aware that I was unconsciously enmeshed in my relationship with her. But acknowledging this and healing from it were two different things. I continued to let her problems distract me from my own growth. It wasn't until she left for California that I finally had to face the self-doubt stuck inside me.

———————

One day, I ran into Mary at the grocery store. We agreed to meet for coffee later that week. She was no longer acting as my sponsor, but we'd decided to remain friends and occasionally took walks together to catch up. When I arrived at our old meeting place, it looked the same. I recognized some of the regular customers and nodded to them as I made my way to a table.

I could hear Malvado whisper, "I wonder what they're thinking about you. Maybe they think you haven't changed much, either." Mary joined me, her eyes crinkling as she sipped her latte. She talked about her work, a concert she was giving, and a recent trip she'd taken to Costa Rica.

"So, how is Olivia? And what's new with you?" Mary asked. I put my cup down and sighed.

"I'm fine, but Olivia isn't returning my calls," I said. "She just sends a quick text now and then." I played with a sugar packet, then tore it open and watched the crystals fall into my latte so I wouldn't have to meet Mary's eyes. "I'm worried she might be in trouble."

"Olivia's living in California now. She's in therapy and going to AA meetings, right? So, she has resources," Mary said. "It's perfectly natural for a daughter to want distance from her mother at this age. Maybe it's as simple as that."

"Yes, but I still worry."

"You will always worry. You're her mother. The problem is you get hooked on worrying then spend hours trying to solve something that can't be solved."

"It makes me sad that she had to move all the way to California to get away from me."

"Why do you think that's the only reason she's moved?"

I looked around the café, glanced out the window to see how many clouds were in the sky, checked my phone. I hated when Mary was right. She had a way of cutting to the core of my resistance, but I never felt judged by her.

"You keep thinking of motherhood as a one-note song," she said.

"What do you mean?"

"You default to the note that says you are too forceful, too opinionated, or offer too much advice."

"Which is true," I said.

"Perhaps. But you've also grown a lot since I've known you."

"So why do I feel so frustrated and depressed about myself?"

"Because you can't let go. Whenever you feel hurt or anxious, you revert to the old story about who you are and blame yourself for being defective. It's more familiar and easier than trusting who you've become. Thinking you are always wrong is the flip side of your mother thinking she was always right. It's the same note."

"Well, that sucks," I said. I could feel a burning behind my eyes, but the heat was too deep for tears. Mary smiled and leaned over the table toward me.

"I'll tell you a secret," she whispered. "It's not all about you." The sun was slanting through the windows, glowing golden. Most of the afternoon customers were leaving as the staff readied tables for the evening crowd. I started to fidget, worried our table would soon be needed for better-paying customers, but Mary locked eyes with me. She had more to say. "Look, you're a strong mother. That can be good or bad. You see the big picture, like a magnificent hawk soaring in the sky surveying the land. But when you want to zero in on a rabbit, you can be merciless. Sometimes, you go after trying to help Olivia with the same intensity. That's who you are. You can try to distract yourself from that or beat yourself up. Or you can use it."

"How?"

"You start by changing your song, the way you perceive yourself. Being a mother involves many complex melodies and chords, and there are lots of ways to play that tune. Take advantage of your strengths and find a new rhythm."

I recognized what Mary was saying. It was the twelfth Step of the 12 Steps. It was the next phase of recovery Tommy Rosen outlined in his book and a familiar theme in Pema Chödrön's lectures: transformation. Transforming pain into something bittersweet but meaningful requires an act of purification, what alchemists called trusting the "secret fire." It is not enough to simply analyze one's suffering. All the therapy, self-help books, and AA meetings won't change things without action. The transformative moment happens when you have the courage and humility to jump into the fire, to let go—not of your child but of your insecurities.

Each stage of motherhood is a new trial by fire, an initiation, a test of determination. Mothers require new skills to understand a child's developmental needs. But rather than support women struggling toward new maternal destinations, our culture blames them for doing too much or too little. As a result, many mothers are uncertain how to transition from parenting a young child to guiding a young adult.

The story of Demeter was helping me see the challenging process of motherhood—and how natural it was to be misguided or unskillful sometimes. My passionate love for my daughter was undeniable. I also recognized how my fear for her safety and my desire to be a good mother were so fierce there was no room for failure and growth. Yet, like many women, I expected myself to be perfect.

For several months, whenever I meditated, I thought about Mary's words and tried to let go. I'd imagine myself at the edge of a high cliff, but my heart would start racing just as I was about to jump in. I'd often end those sessions with a curse word rather than chanting, "Om."

Cultivating Trust

For me, leaping into the void of mothering a troubled teen—like jumping out of an airplane—was an expression of faith. According to theologian Paul Tillich, faith is the state of being "ultimately concerned," which includes an element of doubt. It became my quest to find peace within that doubt.

The way I understand it, one's focus concerning faith can shift or deepen depending on what life presents. For example, when Olivia had suicidal thoughts or battled to give up heroin, I no longer cared how good her grades were or whether she went to college. Instead, I became riveted toward my new ultimate concern: the faith that somehow, she could stay alive.

At first, I pleaded with a God I didn't know, desperately asking for an end to Olivia's suffering—and mine. Then, when relief didn't come quickly enough, I gave up asking for anything at all. I decided to call a woman I knew for advice. She was a Buddhist nun and taught a meditation workshop I'd attended a few years back.

When I entered her home, I could smell a faint scent of sandalwood incense. In the living room, there were several meditation cushions piled in one corner and a framed Tibetan mandala painting hung over the fireplace. When we'd settled on the couch, she asked what was on my mind.

"I'm stuck," I said, as if that explained everything. "I know I need to let go of my fear, but I don't know how to do that skillfully, so I stay stuck."

"Fear is a normal human feeling, like joy or anger," she said. "What's keeping you stuck is the notion that you have to get rid of it. You don't.

But maybe you could look a little deeper to understand what your fear is about."

"My daughter is in addiction recovery, but I'm still afraid of losing her, even though she's fine now. And I can't shake the idea that I'm not a good mother, even though I know that isn't true."

"Listen to you," I heard Malvado hiss. "You sound pathetic." I looked around the room for a clock, thinking I shouldn't be wasting this woman's time. But she was nodding her head as if she understood.

"Letting go is a lifelong pursuit," she said. "Like any journey, it begins with one step and then another. You've got to trust that you are on the right path because there is no other path." Her eyes were kind. I wanted to believe what she was saying.

"So, I just have to trust. There's that word again."

"Trust is a process. Rather than worrying about trust, just try to be at peace right now, in this moment. Don't focus on the past or stress about the future. Accept that you are exactly where you need to be, even if where you are is stuck. Once you can accept that for yourself, your daughter will believe that you can accept her where she is at this moment, too."

"But when I feel stuck, I'm miserable."

"That's your suffering talking. Let's try something. Can you close your eyes and visualize where your body lodges that stuckness?" I sat motionless for a few moments until I sensed my heart squeezing.

"Alright. I have it"

"Good. Describe the sensation. Is it tight, or maybe hot? Does it feel tangled or heavy? Is there a color or texture to it?"

"My heart feels like it's clamping down, becoming paler, weaker."

"Now, allow that feeling to be there, don't try to shut it out. Instead, slowly breathe into it. Then, tell me how you feel."

As I sat, I instinctively put my hand on my heart—the same gesture I'd used so many times to quell the voices of Malvado, the practice I returned to again and again to remember the truth of who I was. I noticed the vice grip inside my chest slowly loosening. I felt my shoulders soften. For a moment, I imagined floating on a gentle wave in the ocean with a brilliant blue sky above me. When I opened my eyes, the Buddhist nun was smiling at me.

"Each moment follows another. What we do with those moments, how we consider them, is what keeps us stuck—or not." We talked some more, and when it was time to say goodbye, I leaned in to hug her but bowed instead. She bowed, then took my hand.

"It takes courage to do what you're doing," she said. "If you keep practicing awareness, you will become more skillful at handling pain when it arises. I can't explain it completely, but you will experience a shift at some point. It's like falling in love. You'll know when it happens."

After our meeting, I started a regular meditation practice. Every morning, I sat on the floor of our living room as shards of sunshine broke through the trees. First, I'd noticed tingling in my feet. The sensation would then travel from my legs to my hips, my core, my heart, and finally, my head. I imagined Persephone reaching up to me from the Underworld, sending her compassion and encouragement. Over time, I began to feel a measure of peace, but it would take a while before I knew what it meant to let go.

DEMETER (RE-IMAGINED)
The Secrets of Eleusis

After weathering Persephone's peril and guiding her daughter to safety, Demeter returned to her goddess duties with more tenderness. No longer needing to charge over the Earth in her fearsome chariot, she shared her sacred wisdom with mortals in a series of secret rites called the Mysteries of Eleusis. Through this storytelling process, Demeter let go of her obsession to protect Persephone. Instead, she focused on helping others move through their fears.

The ceremonies, performed only by women at Demeter's temple, involved reenacting the story of Persephone's descent into the terrifying fires of the Underworld and her triumph over death by ascending again to Earth each spring. Participants learned that death was not an ending but a new beginning. For those who attended, their physical engagement in these ceremonies created a transformation from feeling uncertain to being at peace.

Persephone and Demeter grew closer. The secrets of Eleusis were also the riddles that deepened their relationship. Together, they learned to trust what was natural to the changing cycles of nature and their evolving mother–daughter bonds. The two goddesses reflected on the past and considered the future but made a point of staying focused on the precious time they shared each spring. On warm days, they often enjoyed a cup of ambrosia in an olive orchard that overlooked Lake Pergusa, the spot where Hades had once captured Persephone.

One day, as they sat in the orchard, Persephone asked, "When you dressed up as an old woman in search of me, did you honestly think you would fool anyone?"

Demeter laughed. "I wasn't trying to fool anyone, but I was certainly foolish. I thought making that child into a god would be a blessing—as if being mortal was the only frailty."

"Not even gods and goddesses are impervious to suffering," Persephone said as she unconsciously reached down to rub her ankle.

Demeter noticed the scar that remained on her daughter's leg. Once again, she felt the sharp pain of losing her child to Hades that horrific day. Then, she smiled, remembering how deeply Persephone now loved her husband.

"Or joy," she added.

Returning Home

"Every couple of years, I run away from home," I used to tell my friends. Sometimes, I'd go for a night. Other times, it was longer. It started when I had young children. Henri helped at home when he could, but often he worked late at the hospital. I was exhausted making breakfast, packing lunches, going to work, then driving to dance classes and kayak sessions, arranging playdates, shopping for dinner, feeding the animals, helping with homework, fixing dinner, cleaning up, reading to the kids at bedtime, and talking to Henri after he came home until we crawled into bed.

One time, when the kids were in grade school, I checked myself into a bed and breakfast in Asheville. It was only a few miles from our house. I lugged a cooler with granola, yogurt, berries, deli salads, seltzer, and a bottle of wine up to my room on the second floor of a large Victorian house. The room had a bay window over the front yard. Two oak trees filled my view with bright orange leaves, their giant limbs swaying back and forth as if to music. For two days, I slept, ate, did yoga, read, meditated, and journaled. I wasn't running away—I was returning to myself.

After Olivia hiked the Appalachian Trail and moved to California, I felt that desire again. The years of stress trying to help her recover from addiction had depleted me. I needed to realign myself. Plus, I had a burning desire to return to Seville. There was something there I needed to see.

―――――――――

The taxi driver stopped on a corner, opened the trunk, and pulled out our luggage. "Your hotel is there," he said, pointing down a narrow lane in the middle of the Jewish quarter of Seville. "The street is too small for cars." Henri and I began walking, yanking our carry-on bags over the cobblestones. We'd been hiking along the southern coast of Portugal when I convinced him to make a quick side trip to Seville before going home.

"Seville is a magical place and it's so close. Let's just go for two nights. I think you'd love it." I didn't tell him I had a personal reason for returning.

We found the Hotel Amadeus smashed into the middle of an alleyway. True to its theme, violins, cellos, and harps hung all around the hotel's lobby, and each room had a different classical music name. At the main desk, brochures described churches, parks, theaters, and tours. After we checked in, Henri said he wanted to take a nap. We agreed to meet for dinner. I grabbed a map and my camera, then headed out to the street. As charming as the city was, I had no interest in being a tourist that day. I wanted to find Graffiti Girl.

It had been eight long years since I'd visited Seville with Judy and Pilar, and the chalk image of that little girl had stayed with me. I needed to know what had happened to her. Would I find her image on the same backstreets and alleys, or would she adorn new shop doors and bus stop signs? I walked north, ignoring magnificent museums and palaces as if I was late for a lunch date. I looked for Graffiti Girl, but I only saw pictures of the Virgin Mary. The Mother of All Mothers wasn't just on the sides of churches like before. She was in a tapas bar, on the façade of a hardware store, and in the market among the dead ducks and rabbits all hanging from their delicate ankles. Always perched high on a wall, she looked down on me, crying her bloody tears. I didn't want her pity, so I walked faster whenever I saw her. She was getting on my nerves.

No matter where I looked, I couldn't find Graffiti Girl. Malvado was gone, too. To reassure myself I hadn't just imagined things, I opened my phone and scrolled to the photos I'd kept from my first trip to Seville, checking for shop signs or other clues that might help me find my way to her. As I walked toward the neighborhood where I'd stayed years before, the street corners seemed familiar, but something wasn't right. The boulevard was brighter than I remembered, the buildings sparkling white. I soon realized what had happened. Since I'd last visited Seville, there had been a campaign to beautify the city by removing soot left by decades of pollution. I suddenly remembered reading about it. They'd wiped away all the graffiti, too. It was as if my memories had been scrubbed clean.

I was surprised at how stunned I felt and how much I wanted to cry. I expected Graffiti Girl to be there, still in her youth. But times had changed. She was well on her way, just like Olivia. Perhaps I was just now understanding that my daughter was a woman. I remembered Demeter's depression when Persephone returned to the Underworld. Was Demeter simply sad, or did a part of her disappear each time her daughter left? How was I supposed to retrieve myself and feel whole again?

Passing through the Roman Columns in Alameda de Hercules's tree-lined plaza, I sat down on a park bench and stared at a group of pigeons fluttering around a fountain. *City pigeons only live a couple of years, five or six if they are lucky,* I remember thinking. *These pigeons are the next generation. They are the children or even grandchildren of the ones I used to watch the first time I came to Seville. They never knew Graffiti Girl, and they never knew me.*

I felt dead inside. Despite the sun shining through the trees, a chill passed through me. I took my time walking back to the hotel, feeling foolish for coming to Seville.

Fire as Renewal

The following morning, after walking around Seville, Henri and I returned to the hotel. An ad in the lobby described one-hour music and dance classes offered at Taller, a flamenco school.

"You should definitely do this," Henri said.

"But what about you?"

"I want to go to the Alcazar Palace, which you've already seen."

"Are you sure?"

"Yes, it's simple. You get a singing lesson this afternoon, and we can meet back at the hotel before dinner. When will you get a chance to try something like this again?"

He had a point. And I was curious. For the past several nights, I'd been reading a book about the history of flamenco music and the mystery of what the Spanish poet Federico Garcia Lorca called "duende," a force that comes from a deep, dark place.

Authentic flamenco is not entertainment, the book said. People come to witness the creative triumph of duende. The voice of the flamenco singer is strained, hurting with the agony and confusion of suffering. Struggling for expression in the midst of this pain, the soul surges through the flamenco performer, setting the singer on a creative fire to be purified. If, during the song, the performer has the courage to surrender to the terrifying duende rising through her body, something miraculous happens. Transformation occurs, and beauty is born. The book said that nearly all those who become true flamenco singers do so because it is their fate, their calling. I believed Olivia, too, had been called. Like Persephone, she had to walk through the flames of the Underworld to discover her worth.

I put the book down, turned off the light, and closed my eyes, scanning the years since Olivia stumbled into the kitchen that summer afternoon, seemingly possessed by something dark and frightening. At the time, I didn't understand depression or addiction and didn't know how to help her. However well-intentioned I was, I was afraid of the work she'd have to do, afraid she would burn alive rather than allow the duende to transform her.

Although I eventually learned to trust Olivia's process, I hadn't discovered how to believe in my own. I realized my daughter needed a positive role model, a mother who could forgive herself and express her confidence in life, not only her fear. More than simply letting go of old habits, I wanted to create a new song for myself, one that would honor both my heroics and my fallibility, like the one Homer sang of Demeter.

Outside a two-story building, a hand-painted sign read, "Taller Flamenco," with an arrow pointing skyward. I took my time climbing the rickety stairway. At the top of the second floor, propped in the corner of the cramped reception room, there was a life-sized cardboard cutout of a Spanish woman wearing a full red skirt over multiple lacy petticoats. She was striking a dramatic pose, her right arm raised straight over her head, and her left hand planted firmly on her hip—the quintessential flamenco dancer. Beyond the cardboard figure, there was only one desk in the room. Stacks of sheet music and file folders nearly buried a phone, computer, and young receptionist. I hesitated, wondering if I could turn and bolt down the stairs before she glanced up.

"Hola!" the receptionist said. I stood frozen, trying to remember what in the world made me sign up for a voice lesson in the first place—a flamenco lesson, no less.

"Buenos dias," I said, hoping my accent was passable.

"May I help you?" she asked. Her accent was perfect, while my Spanish was apparently not convincing enough to get past *hello*.

"Are you sure this will work?" I asked.

"What do you mean?" The receptionist tilted her head slightly, still smiling.

"I have a lesson soon, but how will I learn flamenco songs if I can't speak Spanish?" I was feeling even more ridiculous than before.

"Oh, we had a Japanese woman here yesterday who couldn't speak a word of Spanish, and she was fine." I decided to be relieved hearing this.

A full-bodied, middle-aged woman with lovely, thick black hair, heavy eye makeup, and a long skirt made her entrance into the reception area. She didn't smile but gestured for me to follow her. Inside her classroom, the Spanish sun streamed onto a scattering of metal chairs. Nailed to one wall was a giant blackboard. My teacher shut the door behind us. We silently stared at each other for a few awkward moments, then she sighed, went to the blackboard, and started writing Spanish lyrics to a song. I pulled out my camera, planning to record our session, having no other way to practice later what I was about to learn.

"No!" she shook her head many times from side to side, frowning. I understood she did not want her picture taken. Turning the camera around, I pantomimed a question: *Can I at least record the music, no photos?* She considered my request and then slowly nodded in agreement. We began.

My teacher sang the first line of what I assumed was a traditional flamenco song, then gestured that it was my turn. Deeply intimidated, I did my best to repeat it. The notes were easy enough for me to follow, but her intonations were foreign to my ear.

There was no conversation or verbal instruction between us, only music. After practicing a few lines, I relaxed, took a slow breath, and decided to truly listen. With flamenco, words are secondary. Instead, it is the process of singing that frees the soul. Eventually, as the lesson continued, I let go of my inhibitions, opened my throat, and allowed the song to rise from someplace within me. I didn't care who heard me. I closed my eyes and sang my sadness. What came out of my body was the sound of deep torment and frustration—a pain so ancient it was no longer about me. As the song took me far away, I had no awareness of the classroom or the woman in front of me.

When I finished, I opened my eyes and blinked. My teacher seemed somewhat satisfied, though she was not smiling. Flamenco music, she seemed to indicate, is serious business, not easily learned in one session. Still, she nodded her head.

We kept working together as she taught me the song. She would sing a new phrase, then I'd repeat it. What I loved most, and tried hard to imitate, was the sweet sorrow in her voice—a songful lament that embodied anguish and hope but never self-pity. I couldn't quite grasp what the song was about, something having to do with a girl crying out to her mother. It didn't matter. The act of singing flamenco music was working its magic. I felt lighter, lifted. After the lesson, I thanked my teacher, who finally gave me a warm smile, her tutelage completed.

As I walked down a side street toward the plaza, I heard an ambulance wailing in the distance, then a cooing. Looking up, I saw a line of pigeons watching over me from a rooftop. A warm sun caressed my face as dark clouds gathered in one corner of the sky. I caught a hint of fresh baked bread and cigarettes as I passed a café. Everything seemed in balance. Humming the flamenco melody I'd just learned, I kept time by slapping my thighs in counter beats to my steps. For that one moment, I felt something fresh inside, like a spring breeze. I had a new rhythm.

Epilogue

By Olivia

When I finished reading my mother's memoir, I looked at her and said, "This is a love letter to me, isn't it?" We both cried.

Some of it was hard for me to read because I still carry shame about my addiction, and it broke me a little to realize how desperately she wanted to be a good mother. I didn't know my mother struggled with guilt and shame even before my eating disorder surfaced. So, reading about Mom's childhood gave me new insight and compassion for her.

It wasn't always easy growing up in our family. Everyone was successful, and I felt a lot of pressure. Sometimes, I just wanted an escape. When I got too deep into drugs, I knew I needed to change, but I didn't know how. Having my parents' support was crucial to my recovery. It also helped when Mom took responsibility for her actions without blaming herself. It was hard enough trying to stay in control of my feelings. I couldn't handle worrying about hers, too. What strengthened our relationship most was when she dropped the façade of trying to be a perfect mother and could be open and vulnerable with me. That inspired me to take responsibility for my attitude and actions.

Thanks to my community (support groups, friends, and my family), I returned to college, became certified as a health coach, and plan to help others through similar transitions. There will always be challenges, but I am excited about life again.

Acknowledgments

Before I begin my thanks, I acknowledge that I am fortunate in many, many ways. Too often, mothers don't have the resources, support, or medical care so necessary to help their children, let alone help themselves. Too many mothers have lost a child to overdose, suicide, or accidents. It is essential to address the ongoing stigma, misunderstanding, and lack of support related to depression and addiction and to help all caretakers, especially mothers, cultivate compassion for themselves.

As for my journey, I wouldn't have made it without the many women friends (too numerous to list) who cared for me while I cared for my daughter. In particular, I am forever indebted to the Babes (Gail, Pat, and Toone) who helped raise my children and Judy, who propped me up when I couldn't stand. To my college roommate and soul sister, Olivia—I don't know where I'd be without you; Janese, who saved me again and again with her uncanny insights; and Mary, who showed me how to be a better mother. From the bottom of my heart, thank you.

Thanks also go to close friends who took the time to read early drafts of my book. Your love, encouragement, and feedback were so appreciated. To Wilder, Diana, Craig, Judy, Pilar, Helen (you rescued me countless times!), and Callie, my writing buddy, who pushed me to keep going and dragged me to Provincetown twice to work on my book.

I am grateful to those who helped me craft the best version of my memoir, especially Jodie Toohey and everyone at Legacy Book Press who believed in my writing and gave this book wings. Carrie Frye was immensely helpful and supportive in the early stages of developing my ideas, and Jane Huffman expertly edited the final version. Thanks to classics professor Nancy Sultan, who assured me I could add my re-imagining of Demeter to the many versions already in existence, and to Lynn Melnick, who graciously agreed to take time from publishing her own book to help me with mine. To Helen Robinson, who guided me with her keen vision, and Kristen Paulson-Nguyen for her word wizardry. Finally, to Allison Lane, who held my hand and led me through the publication process and beyond.

My greatest appreciation goes to my family. To dear Austin, whose love runs deeper than the ocean—you forever keep me balanced. To Olivia, whose resilience and inner beauty continue to astound me, thank you for allowing me to write my version of our story. And to Henri, for his steadfast love these past forty years and for always encouraging me to grow and create.

Inspiration for writing this memoir came from my resonance with female wisdom and the power to heal ourselves through understanding, acceptance, and connection. When Olivia was dealing with bulimia in high school, she and I read a wonderfully uplifting book called *Eating in the Light of the Moon*. In it, Dr. Anita Johnston illustrates how myth and metaphor have been used for centuries as guidance and instruction in times of trauma.

Through her many books, Pema Chödrön's Buddhist insights deepened my understanding of attachment as suffering, beginning with *The Wisdom of No Escape*, in 1991. Tara Brach's book *Radical Acceptance* showed me how to cultivate self-worth. Tommy Rosen's Recovery 2.0 movement (and the work of others, such as Nikki Myers and Kevin Griffin) add vital positive energy to the conversation about addiction and long-term recovery. To these teachers and to all those advancing the understanding of compassion toward self and others, I offer my humble gratitude.

About the Author

Ann Batchelder writes about women's wisdom and the pain and beauty of difficult transitions. She served as editor of *FIBERARTS Magazine* for ten years. As guest curator for the Asheville Art Museum, she designed and developed three major contemporary art exhibitions featuring internationally recognized artists such as Louise Bourgeois, Ann Hamilton, Sally Mann, Maya Lin, and Laurie Anderson.

In past lives, she earned an English degree from Kenyon College, an MSW in psychotherapy from Simmons University, was Acting Director of the International Studies Program at Lesley University, an account executive for a Manhattan advertising agency, and the Director of Special Events for the Brooklyn Academy of Music. Since 2004, Ann has been practicing mindfulness. The mother of two adult children, she lives with her husband in Asheville, North Carolina. For more information and book group questions: *annbatchelder.com*.